D0909337

Penelope Lively

Twayne's English Authors Series

Kinley Roby, Editor
Northeastern University

TEAS 503

PENELOPE LIVELY
Photo © Jerry Bauer

Penelope Lively

Mary Hurley Moran

University of Georgia

Twayne Publishers • New York
Maxwell Macmillan Canada • Toronto
Maxwell Macmillan International • New York Oxford Singapore Sydney

Penelope Lively

Mary Hurley Moran

Twayne Publishers   Maxwell Macmillan Canada, Inc.
Macmillan Publishing Company   1200 Eglinton Avenue East
866 Third Avenue   Suite 200
New York, New York 10022   Don Mills, Ontario M3C 3N1

Library of Congress Cataloging-in-Publication Data

Moran, Mary Hurley, 1947– .
   Penelope Lively / Mary Hurley Moran.
      p. cm.—(Twayne's English authors series; TEAS 503)
   Includes bibliographical references and index.
   ISBN 0-8057-7028-3
   1. Lively, Penelope, 1933– —Criticism and interpretation. I.
Title. II. Series.
PR6062.I89Z77 1993
823'.914—dc20   93-7655
                                                      CIP

10 9 8 7 6 5 4 3 2 1

Printed in the United States of America.

Once again,
for Mike and Alison,
and in memory of
Mary and Bill Hurley

Contents

Preface

Prior to winning the 1987 Booker Prize for her widely praised novel *Moon Tiger,* Penelope Lively was a virtual unknown in the United States and was known mainly as a children's writer in her native Britain, despite having published six critically acclaimed adult novels. Since 1987, however, her reputation has been catching up with her work, and her adult novels, which now number nine, are being increasingly read and reviewed on both sides of the Atlantic. Furthermore, there are signs that scholars are beginning to take an interest in Lively: in the last few years she has received a number of inquiries from graduate students and professors all over the globe embarking on studies of her work.

One of the intentions of this study is to show that Lively should indeed be regarded seriously by scholars and academics, particularly those interested in the direction the British novel is taking. Her work belies the conventional view that the postwar British novel has reacted against the experimentation of the modernist period and returned to the realism and sociological approach of the Victorian. Despite a certain surface quaintness that causes cursory readers to lump Lively in the "village and vicars" school of British novelists, her fiction explores radical themes about the nature of reality and employs experimental narrative techniques to do so.

In the first chapter I introduce these themes—the interactive relationship between the present and the past, both historical and personal; the dialectic within the individual's consciousness between chronological, or clock, time and psychological time; and the subjective nature of the individual's interpretation of reality—and provide a description of the kaleidoscopic, shifting point of view that characterizes her narrative approach. I also include a biographical account that demonstrates how Lively's thematic preoccupations have grown out of particular formative experiences in her life. Finally, since only the adult novels are dealt with in the body of my study, I briefly survey Lively's short stories and children's fiction, linking them thematically and artistically to the rest of her work. The ensuing chapters explore, via close textual readings, the various ways Lively's characteristic themes and narrative techniques are presented in her nine adult novels to date.

Because virtually no scholarly criticism had been published on Lively's adult novels when I embarked on my research, I have had to rely heavily on book reviews to gain a sense of their critical and popular reception. Another source of information has been general articles about Lively and her work published in British magazines and newspapers. But my most valuable resources have been Lively's unpublished lectures, which she allowed me to photocopy, and the lengthy interview I conducted with the author in June 1990. My interpretations of the novels thus derive mainly from my own close readings and from Lively's own comments about her thematic concerns and intentions.

The purpose of this book, then, is both to elucidate Lively's themes and narrative techniques and to demonstrate that Lively is a sophisticated novelist deserving of wider scholarly attention.

Acknowledgments

I wish to thank Murray Pollinger for granting me general permission to quote from the novels of Penelope Lively and the following publishers for granting permission to quote from the following works: William Heinemann Ltd. for *The Road to Lichfield*, *Treasures of Time*, *Judgment Day*, *Next to Nature*, *Art*, *Perfect Happiness*, and *According to Mark;* Andre Deutsch for *Moon Tiger*, *Passing On*, and *City of the Mind;* Grove Press for *The Road to Lichfield*, *Moon Tiger*, and *Passing On;* HarperCollins for *City of the Mind;* and Dial Press for *Perfect Happiness*.

I wish to thank Penelope Lively for providing me with her photograph, for allowing me to quote from both our personal interview and her unpublished lectures, for patiently and promptly responding to the numerous inquiries I have sent her, and for reading and commenting on the biographical section of the draft of chapter 1.

I would also like to thank the colleagues and friends who have shared with me their responses to Lively's novels, including Sara Baker, Donna Maddock-Cowart, Simon Gatrell, Marianne Causey, Rosemarie Goodrum, and, especially, my aunt Arline Cloney. Special thanks go to my uncle Will Cloney, former sportswriter for the *Boston Post* and former composition teacher at Harvard, for his sharp, sensible editorial advice on chapter 1.

Finally, my deepest gratitude goes to my husband, Mike, and daughter, Alison, whose love, encouragement, and support made this book possible.

Chronology

Chapter One
Lively's Themes, Style, Background, and Other Fiction

Introduction to Lively's Work

Few American readers had heard of Penelope Lively before her seventh novel, *Moon Tiger,* the 1987 winner of England's prestigious Booker Prize, was greeted with superlative reviews on this side of the Atlantic. Her previous novels, although all published in this country as well as in Great Britain, received little attention here. But the success of *Moon Tiger* resulted in a surge of interest in all her earlier books. Lively has subsequently published two more critically acclaimed novels, and is now well on her way to establishing in the United States the kind of literary following she has long been amassing in her native country.

Lively first became known to the British public as an author of children's fiction. Beginning in 1970, she published roughly one children's novel a year through most of the next two decades. These books, most of them charming tales set in cozy rural villages where superstition and legend still have a strong hold, particularly on children, were well received by both reviewers and young readers. Two, *The Ghost of Thomas Kempe* and *A Stitch in Time,* were prize winners (the Carnegie Medal and the Whitbread Award, respectively), with the former having now become something of a classic in children's literature.

Then suddenly in 1977 Lively surprised the public by coming out with an adult novel, and a very fine one at that. *The Road to Lichfield,* praised for its graceful, understated style, its exploration of the way memory operates, and its compassionate portrayal of the dilemmas of middle age, was shortlisted for the Booker Prize. Eight more adult novels and three collections of short stories followed, each favorably reviewed and many receiving awards: the first collection of short stories, *Nothing Missing but the Samovar* (1978), received the Southern Arts Literature Prize; *Treasures of Time* (1979) received the Arts Council National Book Award; *According to Mark* (1984) was shortlisted for the

Booker Prize; and *Moon Tiger,* in addition to receiving the Booker Prize, was shortlisted for the Whitbread Award.

The overriding thematic concern of Lively's fiction is the complex, interactive relationship between the past and the present. Trained as a historian, Lively looks at the world from a historical perspective, always keenly aware of the way the past slumbers in the present. Perhaps the best key to an understanding of the author's ideas on this subject is her one nonfiction book, *The Presence of the Past,* published in 1976 and now out of print. Subtitled *An Introduction to Landscape History,* this work surveys the abundant vestiges of Britain's past that linger in not only its landscape but its architecture, place names, idioms, and so on. Lively continually uses the metaphor of a "palimpsest" to describe this phenomenon, and she expresses her belief in the importance of training one's eye and one's imagination to detect these layers of the past lying just below the surface of the present. She also argues here, as well as elsewhere, for the need to preserve historic landmarks and buildings to confirm the existence of the past. For many of us, Lively believes, history isn't real.

These views are expressed in her fiction usually via protagonists who share her sensibility, who are quick to detect, for example, the pale outline of a Roman road cutting across the modern landscape or the trace of ancient dialect in contemporary speech. Many become involved in historic preservation efforts. Lively does not, however, have the kind of sentimental attitude toward preservation that assumes the past is superior to the present; rather, she believes we must strive for a healthy balance between the modern and the old. We should be equally selective about both preservation and technological development.

Lively is particularly scornful of the contemporary trend of treating the past as quaint and picturesque because she believes it distorts history. In many novels she pokes fun at people who decorate their homes with antique artifacts, ignorant of what the items' original functions even were. She takes an even darker view of those who try to cash in on the contemporary nostalgia for things old, like despicable Toby Standish of *Next to Nature, Art,* who tries to lure guests to his arts workshop program by situating it in his ancestors' rural estate, which he gets up to coincide with the public's idea of life in an eighteenth-century country house.

Equally upsetting to Lively is the prevailing philosophical assumption that we can view history objectively. She argues that for historic events, as for all events, there is no definitive interpretation. In her fiction she tries to convey "the notion that history is fluid, that it is not received opinion but a matter of debate and discussion and interpretation."[1] Furthermore, one's view of historic events is inevitably conditioned by the culture and the period in which one lives. This is the point that iconoclastic historian Claudia Hampton keeps vociferously asserting in *Moon Tiger*. She points out, for example, that the definitive history of Cortez's conquest of the the Aztecs, written by a nineteenth-century Bostonian, is not so much a mirror of Cortez's time as it is "a mirror of the mind of an enlightened, reflective American of 1843. Just as my view [embodied in her own book on the Aztecs] [is] that of a polemical opinionated independent Englishwoman of 1954."[2]

Not only the public, collective past—history—but also the personal past—memory—is of consuming interest to Lively. Just as the outer world is layered, containing vestiges of earlier periods in its landscape, buildings, place names, languages, and so on, so individuals are embodiments of all their younger selves and earlier experiences. Lively has developed a characteristic technique for showing this, by suggesting the potency and fluidity of memory. She typically uses a third-person narrative frame for her story but interrupts this frequently with intimate first-person forays into the main characters' consciousnesses. These exposures reveal the extent to which people live in their memories. Very often an incident in the outer narrative plunges a character into a Proustian re-experiencing of an earlier episode in his or her life. For example, in *Treasures of Time* elderly, maiden Aunt Nellie's experience of pruning her sister's rose garden causes her to recall an emotional moment just after the war when she encountered her future brother-in-law, with whom she was secretly in love, in this same garden. The following excerpt demonstrates Lively's deftness in shifting from the present and the external into the past and the internal:

> And Nellie, intent on a battle with the suckers of a Madame Butterfly in which most advantages were held by the rose, and in her thoughts not present at all, but busy with the reconstruction of this same spot on an afternoon thirty odd years ago, turned at the sound of movement and saw a man standing in the dark frame of the yew.
>
> And there surges that exquisite tide of pleasure, of excitement, of fear. And I say quickly, to cover my feelings because I am very unsure, as yet, what his might be, "It's a lovely garden, Hugh—or at least it will be when you can get it going again, of course it's all in a dreadful mess now."[3]

As the quote indicates, Lively usually switches to present tense when she
has a character relive a memory. The use of this tense, along with the use
of first-person point of view, creates a sense of the immediacy of the
episode recalled, contributing to the impression that memories have a
powerful hold on people's consciousnesses.

Lively's interest in the interactive relationship between past and present necessarily includes a concern with the complexity of time. Lively is
fascinated by the paradoxical nature of this dimension: although we sub-
scribe to the notion that time is objective and chronological, we often
intuit it to be subjective and synchronous. She continually urges this
point in her fiction. For example, by means of characters' insights and
experiences, she suggests that history exists only insofar as there is someone contemplating it; that clock time is merely a human construct, not
an absolute property of reality; that people can experience epiphanic
moments in which they suddenly, gratuitously break free of this construct and apprehend the coexistence of all time; and that human consciousness is a fluid amalgam of memory and awareness of events
occurring in the present—the condition identified by philosopher Henri
Bergson as durational flux.

This interest in the subjective nature of time is part of Lively's larger
interest in the subjective nature of reality in general. Just as all her books
are concerned in some way with the connection between past and present, so do all of them assert to one degree or another her belief that we
always interpret reality in a partial way, according to the particular cargo
of associations, knowledge, and emotional needs we possess; we never—
at least after early childhood—receive reality unfiltered. The major
method Lively uses to vivify this notion is a variation of the modernists'
multiple-points-of-view technique, which can best be described as kaleidoscopic (to use a favorite image of hers) narration. That is, she frequently repeats the same episode two or three times, from each
participant's point of view. Her subtle, almost seamless shift from one
point of view to another can be likened to the shift in patterns that
occurs when a kaleidoscope is rotated: each version of the event, like
each new kaleidoscope design, is different from the preceding one and
yet contains intricate traces of it.

Lively's prose style is characterized by a notable conciseness and
understatedness, which reviewers universally remark upon and praise.
She tends to present episodes in brief, cinematic-like scenarios, usually
with little authorial comment and interpretation, and with meaning and
emotion conveyed by characters' choices of phrase, facial expressions,

and gestures. (It is no doubt this quality of Lively's writing that causes many reviewers to observe that her novels would do well as films, and indeed a number of her works have been, or are being, considered by producers and screenwriters. As of this writing, plans to make a movie version of *Moon Tiger* are in the works.) Lively consciously strives for this kind of compression and has been influenced by novelists who wrote in this same manner. She explains the evolution of her stylistic tastes as follows:

> I grew up—and found books at that voracious point in late adolescence when one reads what there is, before you learn to read as you wish—in the age of the Sitwells, of Norman Douglas, of Lawrence Durrell. A time when the admired literary qualities were those of excess, when language had to be florid, ornate, baroque, elaborate, when you did not use one word where ten would do, when atmosphere and exoticism ranked far above precision or content. I read dutifully but uneasily, knowing that either the times were out of joint or I was. And then I became more adventurous and roamed around and found for myself Henry Green and Ivy Compton-Burnett and others and discovered that the kind of writing I admired was that which aspired to accuracy and realism, that said most by saying least, that employed wit in the proper sense of the word—the precise use of language to convey meaning. . . . I retain my horror of the Sitwells and Lawrence Durrell but am grateful for what I learned from them: to identify my own taste for one kind of writing through aversion from another.[4]

Lively, then, is a conscious stylist. Indeed, one of her avowed reasons for declining to write more children's fiction is that she wanted to experiment stylistically and felt she couldn't do this in children's books: "I realized that my preoccupations were beginning to blossom out into all sorts of concepts that couldn't really be expressed in children's books. They were beginning to demand the sort of stylistic and structural experiment that you can't really inflict on children. Children are marvellous readers, but they are also literary innocents, in that they expect a narrative they're going to follow."[5]

She is not, however, a literary stylist in the sense the term sometimes implies—that is, of being interested only in form and aesthetics. On the contrary, Lively has a very moral view of literature. She believes it can help one with the process of living "by illuminating [life's] conflicts and its ambiguities. We read to find out more about what it is like to be a human being. . . . And one of the things we can do for children, in

books, is just that—expand their vision of a world that is too often root-
ed both in time and place" ("Bones," 643). Furthermore, in an agnostic
age like ours, she feels, literature is "an opportunity to perceive and
explain pattern and meaning in human existence."[6] The writers Lively
admires most, such as William Golding and Edith Wharton, are those
whose fiction engages deeply with moral concerns.

Although Lively believes we are all tethered to a particular time and
place and hence necessarily subjective in our outlooks, she thinks literature can extend our empathy for other points of view. As an author, she
tries to "stick [her] neck out"[7] and write from the perspectives of different kinds of people and situations. Reviewer Helen Chia rightly points
out, "Lively possesses a remarkable ability not only to describe but to
understand a whole range of human emotions. She is an only child but
writes convincingly about sibling relationships; she has enjoyed a stable
marriage . . . for 33 years but can empathise with adulterous lovers in
her novels."[8] And one could add to this list, she is a woman but can
write effectively from a male point of view: three of her novels are cen-
tered around male protagonists and most of the others contain well-
developed secondary male characters. In fact, she takes issue with the
view upheld by some feminists that gender is the ultimate divide: "In a
post-feminist world it is unfashionable to deny the limitations of gender.
We are supposed to be conditioned by them. Men, it has been said, cannot write of women nor vice versa. Frankly, if I thought that I would
both put the cover on my own typewriter and cease to read contemporary fiction" ("Fiction and Reality," 1). Lively thus resists being labeled a
"women's writer,"[9] and although a case can be made for a feminist reading of some of her novels, for the most part her fiction is preoccupied
with concerns other than the situation of being female.

This brings us to the question of where to "place" Lively. Her adult
fiction is too recent to have been included in any of the studies currently
available of the postwar British novel,[10] but they nonetheless help provide an answer to this question. A number of critics point out that
although the reaction against experiment that set in following the period of high modernism continues to dominate the British novel, there
have been signs since the 1960s that some novelists are picking up on
and continuing the experimentalism launched by the modernists.
(Typically cited as examples are John Fowles's *The French Lieutenant's
Woman* and Doris Lessing's *The Golden Notebook*.) But these novelists do
not go as far in this direction as their American and French counterparts.
Rather, they combine technical innovation and formal self-consciousness

with the traditional British novelistic features of plot, character, and satire.

Lively is clearly part of this trend. In her verisimilitude, her concern with character and moral issues, and her incisive social satire, she reveals the influence of Jane Austen and the Victorians; but in her experimentation with point of view, her exploration of the subjective aspects of time and of reality, and her interest in epiphanic moments, she shows a kinship with Virginia Woolf, James Joyce, and T. S. Eliot. And if her seventh and ninth novels are indicative of a developing trend in her writing, she is moving in an increasingly radical direction, replacing chronological plot with spatialization and implying the postmodernist, poststructuralist view that reality is a function of language and of human consciousness. Thus, although reviewers have tended to focus on the "cozy" and "quaint" aspects of Lively's writing (she often sets her novels in old-fashioned villages and includes such stock British types as vicars, spinsters, and committee-attending housewives) and to liken her with Jane Austen and Barbara Pym, this view of her will no doubt change if she continues to produce works like *Moon Tiger* and *City of the Mind.*

Lively's Background

As the preceding assessment of Lively's fiction suggests, this is an author who has been steeped in the English literary tradition. Her love of books began early, spawned in part by the solitary existence she led as an only child growing up far from her native culture. She was born Penelope Low in Egypt on 17 March 1933, the daughter of British nationals Roger Vincent Low and Vera Maud Low (now Greer, née Reckitt). Her father, the son of a Harley Street surgeon, had moved to Egypt as a young man in the late 1920s when job prospects for the professional middle class in England were bleak. He landed a position as assistant to the manager in the National Bank of Egypt, and Penelope's mother went out to join him there a bit later. Although her children's fiction presents vivid pictures of childhood life in British villages, Lively herself spent little of her childhood in England, going there only on brief visits in the 1930s to visit relatives. And once the war started, she did not leave Egypt again until 1945.

Her childhood there was unusual. Her parents were remote figures, and so she spent much of her time with her nurse and the servants. Because there were no schools in and around Cairo that her parents deemed suitable, Penelope had no formal education. Instead, her nurse taught her from a kit developed by the Parents' National Education Union (PNEU) for the children of expatriates living in remote colonies. Her nurse was not particularly well educated, and many of the books and lessons shipped out by PNEU never made it to their destination, so Penelope's was somewhat of a hit-or-miss kind of education. Nevertheless, Lively thinks now that in many ways the PNEU system was the perfect educational method for someone who was to become a writer, for it was devoted almost entirely to narrative and the use of language. The way it worked was that the child would read or have read to him or her a story and then would retell it in writing. The reading list included classic fairy tales and legends, Greek and Norse mythology, and the Old Testament, narratives Lively feels one must be familiar with to fully understand British literature.

The child Penelope loved all this reading. It fed her hungry imagination and kept her company, taking the place of the school friends and siblings she lacked. Despite her solitariness, however, she had a happy childhood (indeed, it took her years to get over her painful longing for Egypt—its sights, smells, sounds, tastes—after she moved away at age 12). The house her family lived in was large and rambling, with a lovely garden containing such exotic creatures as jackals and mongooses. (On her trip back to Cairo in 1984 she discovered to her disappointment that the area had become a crowded, jerry-built slum and the house turned into administrative offices for a technical school.) There were picnics in the desert, outings to the Sphinx and the Pyramids, and yearly visits from a snake charmer who would conduct an elaborate snake-ridding ceremony in the Lows' home.

All through this period World War II was raging just beyond her doorstep, but because Penelope could scarcely remember a time when there hadn't been war, the sight of British troops everywhere and convoys of tanks and armored cars winding through the desert seemed the norm to her. Though she understood very little about what was happening at the time, when she came to write *Moon Tiger,* which is set partly in Egypt during the Rommel campaign, she was aided by the pictures of wartime Egypt she carried around in her head. Similarly, although as a child she knew astonishingly little about Egypt's history, the sense of its antiquity made a deep impression on her imagination. Indeed, Lively attributes her preoccupation with the presence of the past, expressed in all her fiction, to this early exposure to the modern and the ancient existing side by side. She expanded on this point during an interview I had with her in June 1990:

> I can't help but think it [this preoccupation] had something to do with growing up in as temporally complex a place as Egypt, which juxtaposes time in the most extraordinary way, I mean in the sense that you have Pharaonic and Mameluke and Turkish remains and Greek and Roman all coexisting, so that there seems to be no sequence of time. And as a child I didn't really understand this, because I was never taught any history—rather surprisingly, no one ever seemed to teach me much about the history of the country I was living in. But you couldn't escape seeing this, and a sort of contemplative little girl, as I suppose I must have been, couldn't help but observe that here was all this coexistence of different times. So I think that may well have had something to do with it—this perplexed recognition that here was a complete muddle of a place in which centuries all seemed to coexist without any structure. And I suspect that at some point this somehow got translated into a recognition that, after all, the same thing goes on in terms of personal life, that one's memory is not in any sense a chronological or linear thing but that in the head everything happens at once. I think analogies of this kind might have sprung from growing up in such a place.[11]

This sensibility was further developed when she moved to England, where antiquity and modernity also coexist, albeit not so dramatically as in Egypt. She describes an experience she had as an adolescent when she visited Cheapside in the City of London and was suddenly flooded with an almost visionary awareness of the past: "The bombs have stripped the landscape down to its origins: the medieval street plan, the exposed bastions of the Roman wall. Time is lying there in front of me, but I cannot make head nor tail of it. . . . I have never been to school or read any history. . . . But something happens to me, standing there in the rubble, looking at old walls. I am excited; I am lifted out of the prison of my own head and glimpse something larger. Imagination reaches out" ("Bones," 642). She goes on to reflect, "Awareness of the past, it seems to me, is an achievement of the imagination. In my own case it was prompted first by this kind of experience—a response to the physical world, a perception of things not understood but recognized, a child's amazed vision of the layered world" ("Bones," 642). The seeds of her literary imagination, then, were sown in these early quasimystical experiences in Egypt and England.

In contrast to her happy, contented childhood, Lively's adolescence was bleak. The war over and her parents on the verge of divorce, it was decided that Penelope should return to England and stay with her widowed paternal grandmother, who lived in a six-story house on London's

Harley Street. The windows of the house had been blown out in the blitz, and Lively recalls how a sense of disorientation and uprootedness suddenly overtook her when she had to wade down the stairs through snow that had drifted in through the broken windows: "this for a little girl who'd been brought up in Africa" (Interview).

When her father returned to England (her mother remarried soon after the divorce and after a few years of living in London, moved to Malta, where, now in her early 90s, she still resides), he decided it was high time Penelope received some formal education, so he abruptly dismissed her nanny and packed her off to boarding school. Although Lively can now sympathize with his reasoning, at the time his actions struck her as cruel. In writing *Going Back* she no doubt drew upon her memory of the horror of being ripped from the cozy, nurturing existence she'd led with her nanny and hurled into a cold, uncongenial boarding school. In the novel a boy and his younger sister enjoy an idyllic childhood living in their rambling country home with a kindly, indulgent housekeeper while their widowed father is away at war. When he returns and announces his decision to send the boy away to school, the two children plummet into a profound depression, and the boy's life at boarding school turns out to be a kind of purgatorial existence.

The same was true of Lively's own experience at a school in Seaford, on the coast of Sussex. It was a philistine place, with emphasis on sports rather than academics, the kind of institution that produces girls like the Norton-Smith sisters in Lively's children's novel *The Wild Hunt of Hagworthy:* physically healthy and outdoorsy but narrow-minded, class-conscious, and unintellectual. Penelope was a misfit because she was not good at athletics and because she read *The Oxford Book of English Verse* while the other girls preferred Mills and Boon romances. In fact, the administration's idea of punishment was to send the offending pupil to the library for an hour to read a book! So intellectually repressive was the school that Lively shudders to think how she would have turned out if she'd been sent there at age 7 instead of 13—she's sure she would not have ended up a writer.

Throughout her adolescence, Lively felt herself very much an outsider, almost a refugee. She was bewildered by the tacit, Byzantine social rules she encountered in England. One of her more autobiographical short stories, "A Clean Death," is based on an experience she had visiting her aunt's (her father's sister's) family in East Anglia over the Christmas holidays. Like the 14-year-old protagonist, young Penelope went off hunting one morning with a neighborhood boy of her own age that she'd befriended. Upon returning to the house, she was met with a display of coldness and annoyance on the part of her aunt and uncle. At the time she assumed that they, being great animal lovers, were expressing their disapproval of her killing a rabbit, but gradually it dawned on her that what they were really disapproving of was her socializing with a boy of a lower class. She had unwittingly committed a social taboo. *The Wild Hunt of Hagworthy* also draws on Lively's adolescent experience of social confusion: the 12-year-old protagonist, en route to spend the summer holidays at her aunt's in the country for the first time since age 7, looks forward to playing with her old group of friends there, but upon arriving discovers that they no longer socialize with one another because of their growing awareness of the differences in their class backgrounds.

Not all Lively's boarding school holidays, however, were miserable. She had some happy experiences visiting her beloved maternal grandmother in West Somerset, a kindly old woman who was probably responsible for the deep affection for old people one senses in Lively's fiction. It was during her time spent with her grandmother that a couple of key experiences in Lively's intellectual and cognitive development occurred. One was the birth of her conscious interest in history. She'd been in the habit of accompanying her grandmother and aunt, both great architecture buffs, on tours of old country churches and cathedrals. Like most teenagers, she found this kind of activity intensely boring, and would generally be preoccupied with daydreaming or thinking about her next meal while she traipsed around behind her relatives. But on one such occasion she had a kind of epiphany in which she suddenly grasped the reality of history. She described this experience in our interview: "I remember one of those Virginia Woolf-like moments of vision, moments of truth, in one of these churches, looking at one of those stone effigies of the knight and the lady, which is so common a feature of English churches, and I'd never really *looked* at it before—I'd seen hundreds of them and been bored to tears by them—and suddenly looking at it and getting this sort of revelatory moment of 'But this is true; there were actually people like this; this actually happened'" (Interview). This experience, which she later fictionalized in her children's novel *The Stained Glass Window,* launched her lifelong interest in history and in the whole topic of the difficulty of seeing the past clearly. It was also the root cause of her decision to read history when she got to Oxford.

The other formative experience that occurred during these visits with her grandmother was the crystallization of Lively's religious—or nonreligious—outlook. Lively had a conventional Church of England upbringing, attending church and saying her prayers regularly. But whereas her parents paid mere lip service to religion, her maternal grandmother was a real believer. In the course of their holidays together adolescent Penelope, who had begun to feel the stirrings of agnosticism within her, from time to time engaged her grandmother in religious discussions. She recalls one argument in which she tried to convince her grandmother that agnostics are just as moral as Christians, the only difference being that the former do not base their moral system on a belief in the existence of God or an afterlife. Penelope went through the Ten Commandments with her grandmother, pointing out that she agreed with and tried to live according to almost all of them. It was this experience of debating theological points with a believing Christian that helped Lively articulate and solidify her emerging agnosticism. And her agnosticism, along with the secular humanism and the existential anxiety it gives rise to, is expressed in nearly all her novels.

After three years in boarding school, Lively was finally rescued by her father, who had begun to perceive the academic deficiencies of the place. He pulled her out and sent her to a "crammers—a school for cramming what hadn't got into one's head before."[12] There she stayed from age 16 to 18, when she went off to St. Anne's College, Oxford, to study history. This was 1951.

Lively's university years contrasted markedly with her miserable adolescence. For the first time she had an active social life—perhaps too active, she now thinks:

> I was rather frivolous: very sociable, but with quite the wrong sort of people—wrong in the sense that I wouldn't have anything in common with them now. Rather hearty types—rowing men and so on. No doubt they're horrified at how I've turned out. I realize now that I should have been doing things on *Isis* and all sorts of journalism, but it didn't occur to me then. Ironically, some of my closest friends now are people who were my contemporaries at Oxford, but I never knew them when I was there. (Hardyment, 30)

Caught up in social activities, she was not an assiduous student and claims not to have received a very good degree. Despite this, the seeds of her intellectual and creative interests were sown during her period at Oxford. Looking back, she now realizes that "although I had no idea of what was happening at the time, reading history totally formed me. It didn't make me a novelist, but it determined the kind of novelist that I have become. It formed a climate of mind" (Hardyment, 30).

At the time, however, she had no thoughts about a career as historian or novelist—or anything else, for that matter. Curiously, women of her generation graduated from university "equipped both for everything and nothing" (Interview). They were highly educated, yet not expected to pursue careers. In fact, the Appointments Board at Oxford, from which students sought employment advice in their final year, routinely urged women to take a course in shorthand and typing immediately after graduation, for "if you couldn't also do shorthand and typing, nobody was going to employ you even if you had a good Oxford degree. And of course if you had shorthand and typing abilities you then found yourself being a secretary" (Interview).

Lively docilely followed this advice, moving into her father and stepmother's home in London and embarking on a routine of tutoring a couple of children in the mornings, attending secretarial school in the afternoons, and looking for a job in her spare moments. After about six months of this she was offered and accepted the position of research assistant for the professor of race relations at St. Antony's College, Oxford. Although she found the college immensely stimulating, the job itself was a dead end, and in retrospect she thinks that if she hadn't gotten married within two years she probably would have "felt restive and gone into something else or started to behave more sensibly about having a career of some kind. . . . I would have liked teaching, I think" (Interview).

But as it was, after about a year at this job she met Jack Lively, who had come to Oxford from Cambridge as a junior research fellow in politics, and they married within six months, in 1957. Her life then assumed a very traditional shape, as she proceeded to have two children right away and become a full-time housewife and mother.

These were happy and important years for Lively. For one thing, motherhood proved to be deeply satisfying for her. In a rebellion against her own childhood, in which she was looked after by servants, Lively threw herself into caring for Josephine, born when she was 25, and Adam, born three years later. Motherhood, she claims, is the one experience she wouldn't have missed. The intensity of her feeling is reflected in many of her female characters, who are prone to surges of overwhelming maternal tenderness, as when their gaze lights upon their young child playing in the yard or when they suddenly catch a glimpse of the baby face hovering just beneath the surface of their adolescent child's face.

These years were also important for Lively because they gave her the opportunity to immerse herself in literature. Having studied history rather than English at Oxford, she felt there were gaps in her reading and spent her baby-minding years catching up: "My memory is of trundling a pram with two children in it every day to the public library to get more books. I read my way through twentieth-century literature, as it were, stirring the baby food with one hand and holding a book in the other" (Interview). Looking back today, she finds this phase of her life curiously paradoxical, in that full-time motherhood was very restricting but at the same time immensely liberating "because since I wasn't working I had this opportunity in every spare moment to do an enormous amount of reading" (Interview).

She believes that this intensive reading for a period of about eight years caused her to grow and change a great deal, to the extent that she became serious about wanting to do something more with her life once her children no longer needed as much attention. Consequently, as soon as Adam started school—quite literally the first day he went off—she sat down and began to write. Having read a great deal of children's fiction to her children, she was fascinated by this genre and wanted to try her hand at it. Her first attempt was, by her own assessment, "the most awful historical novel" (Interview), which was never published and which she has since thrown out. But her second attempt, *Astercote* (1970), was accepted for publication immediately.

From that point on Lively was a full-time author, writing all day while her children were at school and publishing roughly a book a year. During these years the family moved around quite a bit as her husband pursued his academic career, beginning with a three-year assistant lectureship at the University of Swansea, when the children were preschoolers, and moving on to jobs at Sussex, then Oxford, and finally, in 1978, to a chair at the University of Warwick, which he held until his recent retirement. Lively, who is very aware of the role that fate and luck play in one's life, modestly asserts that had she not been married and had a breadwinner husband, she might well not have become a successful writer, for she would have had to worry about earning a living. Although her early novels were all well received and translated into several languages, it was not until about eight or nine years ago that she could have supported herself solely by her writing.

Today Penelope and Jack Lively divide their time between their seventeenth-century stone farmhouse near Chipping Norton, Oxfordshire, and their townhouse is Islington, North London, not far from which reside Josephine and Adam, both of whom are married. Josephine, the mother of two small daughters, is a free-lance professional oboist, and Adam is a writer who has published three novels.

Lively and her husband generally spend their days writing—Jack Lively has published several books on political theory—and, when at their country home, gardening. In addition to novel writing, Lively does a considerable amount of journalism and book reviewing, writes occasional radio and television scripts, has acted as a presenter for a BBC radio program on children's literature, and travels and lectures for the British Council. She is a fellow of the Royal Society of Literature, chairperson of the Society of Authors, and a member of PEN. Since the publication of *Moon Tiger* and its subsequent wildfire acclaim, she has also been doing a great deal of traveling, the result of invitations to give readings and talks throughout the world.

Despite her success, Lively remains unassuming and down to earth, not unlike the no-nonsense, unpretentious women that people her novels. Indeed, she has no patience with successful writers who become taken with themselves and "strike up attitudes, who think that being creative gives them a license to behave badly. A writer may have a special skill but he is no different from other people" (Chia, 2).

The blend of modesty, astuteness, and crusty wisdom expressed in this sentiment constitutes the voice that so many readers find appealing in all her novels.

Children's Fiction

Lively took children's literature seriously long before it became academically fashionable to do so. She read extensively to her own children right up until their teens, and in the process developed an increasing appreciation for and interest in this genre. She prefers traditional children's fiction over the kind of didactic realistic fiction, more common in the United States than in Great Britain, that serves as "an instrument for social engineering and a platform for benign instruction about how to cope with divorce, the inner cities, racism, sexism and any other ills of our day."[13] The kind of children's literature Lively values is that which enters into the way children look at the world, that which employs fantasy and questions the assumptions adults bring to bear in their perception of reality: "Such writing recognises the child's own unconstricted vision. Why shouldn't animals talk? As adults, we live within the straitjacket of accepted and defined reality; the child does not. Each child sees the world freshly, without preconceptions and without assumptions; the best writing for children, while incapable of recovering that vision, can at least acknowledge and respect it" (Exhibit Brochure).

In her own juvenile fiction Lively uses elements of fantasy to interest youngsters in the same general theme she presents in her adult fiction: the intricate connection between the past and the present. She believes that it is particularly important to awaken children to the reality of history, because "without such awareness [they are] blinkered, confined by self."[14] She is not a historical novelist in the conventional sense, however (and in fact is critical of most historical novels for children, which she says tend to treat the past as costume drama). All her books, with one or two exceptions, have contemporary settings but involve the protagonist's becoming sensitive to the subtle echoes from the past that reverberate in his or her environs. Whereas in her adult novels this sensitivity arises from an act of the imagination, in her children's novels it is usually caused by supernatural phenomena—ghosts, poltergeists, and time warps. Lively believes this is an effective way to present her theme, since for children "the borderline between fact and fantasy is . . . shadowy. . . . Suspension of disbelief is a natural part of childhood; what is real and what is imagined, what happens and what does not, are hardly divided. It is only later that we are supposed to be sure of these distinctions" ("Bones," 645).

Although Lively's children's books range in tone and style from the comic and lighthearted to the poetic and brooding, and although they appeal to a range of age levels, one could describe her typical juvenile novel as follows. The protagonist, aged about 10 or 12 and dwelling in a quaint English village, becomes aware of the occurrence of a supernatural phenomenon, usually some kind of manifestation of something from the village's past, and attempts to solve the mystery or problem this creates. In doing so, the child usually forms an alliance with one or two other children and an open-minded, sympathetic elderly adult (often a grandparent), and this little band must contend with the disbelief of the rational-thinking adults in the community (including usually the protagonist's parents). Ultimately the children succeed in resolving the situation or banishing the menace, but only they know that they are the heroes: the narrow-minded adults attribute some other, logical cause to the resumption of normalcy in the village. Generally these tales are told by a third-person narrator who seems to have an affectionate and humorous understanding of children and of the scrapes they so often find themselves in.

The prototype of the above sketch is the prize-winning novel *The Ghost of Thomas Kempe.* This tale was in good part inspired by Lively's reading of Keith Thomas's landmark work *Religion and the Decline of Magic* (1971), a book that made a strong impression on Lively and, according to her, changed a lot of people's thinking about history and helped gain academic respectability for the study of history of ideas. Massively researched, *Religion and the Decline of Magic* is at heart an attempt to get people to take seriously—rather than regard as simply quaint or ignorant—the nonscientific world view of sixteenth- and seventeeth-century England.[15] In *The Ghost of Thomas Kempe* Lively juxtaposes the seventeenth century and the twentieth, with the intention of underscoring the relative, culturally biased nature of their respective explanations of natural phenomena.

A humorous narrator with an obvious soft spot for ebullient little boys who are always being blamed when things go wrong tells the story of 10-year-old James Harrison. Soon after he and his family move into a 300-year-old cottage in the village of Ledsham, strange things begin to happen: objects fly about the house or are mysteriously misplaced, and angry notes written in seventeenth-century script suddenly appear on James's desk and elsewhere in his home. James is accused of carelessly breaking objects and of writing notes to gain attention. He knows that it is futile for him to try to convince his parents of what he gradually pieces together is the real cause of all this disruption: the ghost of Thomas Kempe, a sorcerer who lived in the cottage three centuries earlier, is disturbed by many of the "newfangled" goings-on and modern scientific beliefs of the villagers and so has emerged from his grave to protest loudly, aiming to enlist James as his assistant.

Discovering a cache of old letters and diaries that his parents had thrown out when clearing out the attic, James is fascinated to learn that a boy of his own age named Arnold Luckett had had this same experience in the middle of the nineteenth century while visiting his aunt, who owned the cottage then. As he reads through all this material, James begins to feel a kinship with the boy and his sympathetic aunt, who, unlike James's parents, was completely accepting of Arnold's theory about a ghost haunting the house. James becomes intrigued by the idea of having a "friendship" that cuts through the dimension of time. Arnold even helps James resolve his crisis by letting him know, via the diaries and letters, how he had resolved his own: through exorcism. With the aid of a local carpenter who secretly practices exorcism, James eventually succeeds in getting Thomas Kempe to return quietly to his grave.

In this novel Lively thus suggests to young readers "something of the palimpsest quality both of people and of places, those layerings of memory of which both are composed" ("Bones," 644), while also opening their eyes to the reality of the past and of earlier people's ways of regarding the world. The same intention underlies most of her other juvenile novels, and always it is only children, with the occasional exception of an imaginative adult ally, who are sensitive to the manifestations of the past. Thus, for example, in *Astercote* 12-year-old Mair Jenkins is flooded with visions of fourteenth-century village scenes whenever she finds herself in the vicinity of the deserted medieval village that once existed in what is now a tract of forest adjacent to the modern housing estate where she lives. And in *The Whispering Knights* three children and an old lady they befriend are the only ones in the village to perceive that a suspicious-looking newcomer who is influencing her tycoon husband to route a proposed superhighway through their village, thereby destroying many ancient buildings and landmarks, is actually a modern-day transfiguration of the medieval witch Morgan le Fay. Believing the local legend that a Stonehenge-like circular arrangement of ancient stones on the outskirts of the village was once a troop of knights who successfully fought a bad queen, and that the spot is therefore anathema to evil, they lure the woman there and, sure enough, she vanishes.

A number of Lively's other children's novels present similar situations in which the protagonists are forced to acknowledge the reality of the past. These include *The Driftway, The Wild Hunt of Hagworthy* (published in the United States as *The Wild Hunt of the Ghost Hounds*), *A Stitch in Time, The Revenge of Samuel Stokes,* and *The Stained Glass Window.* In many of these the protagonists also gain an appreciation of different ways of looking at the world, just as James Harrison comes to realize that sorcery, astrology, and alchemy made as much sense in the seventeenth century as modern science dies in the twentieth. Lively's intention of helping youngsters expand their understanding of other points of view is most apparent in *The Driftway.* The protagonist, Paul, decides to run away to his grandmother's because he cannot accept his widowed father's new wife. Hitchhiking, he is picked up by a junk cart driver named Bill, a wise old man who immediately intuits the boy's problem and who in the course of their journey helps him to escape the prison of self. Bill travels off the main road along a grown-over grassy lane known as "the driftway," which cattle droves traveled to market centuries ago. He tells Paul about the mystical experiences he had as a boy on this same road, and soon Paul himself begins to have such experiences:

visions in which people who had traveled this route in the distant past suddenly appear and speak to him. Sometimes these visions involve a group of people who were all present at the same event but who each have a different version of it to report. The result of all these exposures to the outlooks of different periods and to multiple accounts of the same event is that Paul is forced to consider how subjective his own point of view has been. Ultimately his understanding and sympathy are enlarged and, realizing how narrow-minded he has been about his father and new stepmother, he returns home.

Closely related to Lively's theme of the importance of being aware of the past, of course, is her focus on the mysterious nature of time. This is a major concern in her adult fiction, but it also lends itself peculiarly well to her children's fiction because time is "a subject provocative to children, poised so precariously at the brink of life and perplexed about its direction, and about their own place in the scheme of things" (Exhibit Brochure). James Harrison, whose friendship with a boy who lived over a century earlier is as vital and real to him as any of his other relationships, discovers that the past is not something dead and gone but something that can be evoked through emotions and imagination. In *A Stitch in Time* 11-year-old Maria has a similar insight when she finds herself feeling closer and closer to the little girl she learns lived in her family's rented summer cottage 100 years earlier and slept in the same bedroom Maria now sleeps in. The linearity of time dissolves for Maria—as it does for James—as the past becomes as real to her as the present.

Another young protagonist who is fascinated with the nature of time is 14-year-old Clare Mayfield of *The House in Norham Gardens*. Growing up in her family's ancestral home, she has become aware of the way a house can embody the lives of its previous inhabitants, in a sense trapping pockets of time within its walls. An orphan, Clare is raised by two sprightly elderly aunts whose views enhance her appreciation of the non-linearity of time: original thinkers, they are always making comments about how one's head is a storehouse of time and how it is artificial to fence people off according to age.

When Clare discovers in a trunk in the attic a primitive shield once belonging to her anthropologist grandfather, she begins to study the New Guinea tribe that produced it and is fascinated to learn that chronological time does not exist for them; lacking the concepts of history and the future, they dwell in an eternal present. The fact that this tribe is still living in the Stone Age while most of the rest of the world is experiencing the late twentieth century contributes further to Clare's developing belief that time is a relative rather than an absolute and chronological phenomenon. This novel's structure—the main narrative about Clare and her life with her aunts in North Oxford is interspersed with accounts of the simultaneous goings-on in a primitive New Guinea village—and content are more sophisticated than those of most of the other children's books, making it more appropriate for the oldest children in Lively's juvenile audience range (roughly 12- to 15-year-olds).

In both *The House in Norham Gardens* and her next book, *Going Back,* which have been likened respectively to the fiction of Marcel Proust and Virginia Woolf,[16] Lively indulged in the kind of narrative and stylistic experimentation that would eventually characterize her fiction for adults and which she ultimately decided was not appropriate for children's literature. Although all of Lively's children's books are appealing to adults, these two novels, with their lyrical prose and their technical complexity, are particularly so. Indeed, her publisher has recently decided to switch *Going Back* from the juvenile to the adult literature category.

In retrospect this novel appears to be a warm-up for Lively's first adult novel, published two years later. Her focus in *Going Back* is on psychological time and the workings of memory. The protagonist, a middle-aged woman named Jane, returns one last time to her childhood home to collect some belongings before the house is sold. This is the occasion for a number of intricate Proustian flashbacks to childhood experiences, all presented in the kind of present-tense, first-person scenes Lively uses in so many of her adult novels. Woven into all these flashbacks are the adult Jane's musings about the way memory is always subjective. Although the vivid evocation of a rural English childhood may appeal to young readers, the real subject of the book—the way our adult consciousness imposes itself on our memories, making it impossible for us to recall exactly the way the world looked to us as children—is probably of greater interest to adult readers.

In addition to the children's books concerned with history, time, and memory, Lively has produced a number of others that are thematically less weighty and generally geared to younger children (the 8- to 10-year-old range). Some center around talking animals, and in these Lively is perhaps at her cleverest and most humorous. She is clearly a keen observer and lover of animals, particularly dogs (one senses this in her adult fiction, too, which contains some vividly portrayed pets), and can brilliantly and comically capture various animals' characteristic gestures and attitudes. *The Voyage of QV66* is a lighthearted fable about a motley group of animal friends who set off on a lengthy journey in search of the relatives of one of them—a monkey who has never seen another of its kind. They meet with various dangers and obstacles on their voyage but ultimately make it to their destination, the London Zoo. At the same time that she narrates an exciting tale sure to captivate young readers, Lively also opens their eyes to a range of points of view as she shows how differently the various animals react to the same events. Older readers no doubt appreciate the tale's underlying satire, by means of which Lively uses the animals to represent various character types—for example, she gives us a scrappy streetwise dog, a pragmatic horse devoid of imagination and intellectual curiosity, a vain cat preoccupied with her own comfort and appearance, and so on—and to expose some of the illusions and vanities human beings are prone to. The allegory never becomes heavy-handed, however, and the animals remain fully realized "characters."

A House Inside Out is a delightful collection of tales about the animal creatures who inhabit the house of a family named Dixon. Each of the 11 stories is told from the point of view of one of the animals and recounts a noteworthy adventure the animal has had in the house. All of this goes on, of course, unbeknownst to the Dixons, who attribute such mishaps as broken teapots and misplaced candle-holders to either the naughtiness of the family dog, Willie (the only animal the Dixons are aware they share their home with), or some other reasonable cause, when in fact the real culprits are usually among the other creatures—spiders, woodlice, mice, and a pigeon—who dwell under their roof. A humorous, ingenious book, it displays once again Lively's characteristic flair for opening young readers' eyes to varying points of view and suggesting that rational adult analysis of situations is often limited.

Lively has written a handful of short, easy-to-read, heavily illustrated books for very young readers (the seven- to nine-year-old range). Some of these are set back in time. *Boy without a Name,* for example, is set in the seventeenth century and concerns an orphan who is ignorant of the world: he doesn't know how to read, doesn't know that the country he lives in is England, and doesn't know the names of a great many things. Once again, Lively's aim seems to be both to help children imagine what the historical past was really like and to expose them to a way of looking at the world that is very different from their own.

The *Fanny* books—*Fanny's Sister, Fanny and the Monsters,* and *Fanny and the Battle of Potter's Piece*—are also set in an earlier period, the mid-nineteenth century. In charming and vivid detail, Lively describes life in a rambling Victorian household, complete with nurseries and nannies and cooks and a large brood of children, reminiscent of the Pockets in

Great Expectations. At the center of all three books is nine-year-old Fanny, the eldest of the eight Stanton offspring. She is an endearingly real little girl who is always getting into scrapes because of her tomboy ways and her annoyance with the string of new babies who keep usurping her place in Nurse's affections and on Nurse's lap.

The remaining works in the easy-to-read category—*Dragon Trouble, Debbie and the Little Devil,* and the tales included in *Uninvited Ghosts and Other Stories*—have contemporary settings and generally involve protagonists who become aware of supernatural or anthropomorphic phenomena going on in their home, such as dragons living in a tunnel beneath the bedroom, a mischievous devil disrupting the household, a martian landing in the backyard. As in the more serious variations of this theme in the books for older children, it is the child who must resolve the situation, because rational adults are incapable of detecting the supernatural—except, of course, for the sympathetic grandparent or elderly person who figures in many of these works.

In these tales, as in all of her children's fiction, Lively reveals her deep understanding of and respect for the way children look at the world, deriving from her "uncannily accurate and honest recall of what it is like to be a child in a world made for adults" (Egoff, 41). Her popularity with young readers (she continues to receive numerous letters from them every week) no doubt stems from their sense that here is an author who takes them seriously, who is not out to socialize them or mold their thinking. Although she now concentrates on works for adults, she claims to be "intensely interested in children still" (Hardyment, 30) and maintains an extensive library of children's fiction in her London home.

Short Stories

For Lively the process of writing children's fiction is similar to that of writing short stories.[17] Both require "the same sort of accuracy and economy. There is some room for manoeuvre in a novel—what Graham Greene calls linking passages. There's no room for manoeuvre in either a short story or a children's book" (Hardyment, 31). Although lately Lively's full schedule has made it difficult for her to find the stretches of blank time, or "bits of tranquillity in life" (Hardyment, 31), required for the concentrated effort of producing a short story, she is insistent about wanting to continue writing this genre, to which she is as much devoted as she is to the novel. "I certainly think of myself very much as a short story writer," she claims, "and want to be doing that and feel irritated that I'm not because other things crowd in" (Interview).

She has been writing short stories sporadically since her early days as an author. Her first 14 were published in 1978 as a collection entitled *Nothing Missing but the Samovar.* Her subsequent stories have appeared in various periodicals, including *Encounter, Vogue, Cosmopolitan, Good Housekeeping,* and the *Literary Review.* In 1984 the 11 stories she had written since *Nothing Missing but the Samovar* were collected and published as *Corruption,* and in 1986 an omnibus volume containing all 34 of her stories to date (including those appearing in the first two collections) was published as *Pack of Cards.*

Although she uses many of the same character types and settings in both genres, Lively's stories are in some ways very different from her novels. Whereas the novels are heavily thematic and intellectual, as discussed earlier, most of the stories are more like little slices of life. The reader is left with a rich impression of a moment in the protagonist's experience rather than with a sense of the story's "meaning." In this respect her stories have something of the quality of memories: pungent and evocative but not clearly definable. Indeed, she claims that

> in its very structure the short story has an eerie relationship with the processes of memory. . . . It holds up for inspection an incident, a relationship, a situation . . . and draws therefrom, either obviously or in some quite oblique manner, a significance. It may carry resonances about events beyond the parameters of the story, but it is self-contained: within its own circumference it tells us all we need to know, if it is doing its job properly. And is that not a paradigm for a memory? An episode within the mind which appears in isolation, significant perhaps in a wider context, but complete in itself. ("Fiction and Reality," 15)

Lively draws on personal memories for many of her short stories and claims that for her this genre is more directly autobiographical than is the novel. In particular, the experience of feeling displaced when she was uprooted from Egypt to England as an adolescent seems to haunt her, for she has transformed it into a number of stories. Probably the most autobiographical of these is "A Clean Death," discussed earlier, the thinly veiled account of her boarding school holiday spent with relatives whose disapproval she incurred for not being familiar with the tacit social rules of Britain's rural gentry. In spare yet suggestive prose Lively creates a vivid impression of the bewilderment, awkwardness, and intense loneliness that 14-year-old Carol, the protagonist, feels in this alien culture, far from her beloved India.

Another tale that portrays the situation of being an outsider is "Nothing Missing but the Samovar," about a young German graduate student who is in England to do his political science thesis on nineteenth-century Anglo-Prussian relations. While there he is invited to stay with a Dorset family in possession of papers helpful to his study. Like the scholarly protagonist of *According to Mark,* whose research also entails his holing up in someone's private home for a spell, Dieter becomes emotionally enthralled by the family he stays with. His growing enchantment with them and with the English way of life—its people, its landscapes, its village customs—reflects Lively's own experience of falling in love with England. In reaction against her initial feeling of alienation, she developed a profound desire to put down roots in her adopted country, and nearly all her fiction reveals her deep attachment to English life and landscape.

A number of stories in addition to "A Clean Death" explore adolescent moral and social confusion, albeit not always precisely of the sort Lively herself experienced. For example, "The French Exchange" portrays a teenager who for the first time senses the hollowness and philistinism of her way of life when she becomes acquainted with an intellectual French exchange student. Again, in "The Darkness Out There" a teenaged girl is deeply disturbed by her sudden realization that the sweet, grandmotherly old lady she has been visiting as part of her school's Good Neighbors program is capable of evil: in the course of one visit the woman blithely recounts to Sandra an episode during the war when a German plane crashed down near her rural cottage and, still bitter from having lost her husband to the German enemy, she took vindictive pleasure in leaving the trapped survivor there to die. For Sandra the hitherto sunny, comprehensible world has suddenly become a morally murky place.

The stories discussed thus far focus on the emotional state of the protagonist and are narrated in a traditional third-person omniscient fashion. Absent are the characteristic themes about history, memory, and time and the experimental narrative techniques that characterize Lively's novels. In a handful of her stories, however, Lively adumbrates some of these themes and techniques. An early story entitled "Interpreting the Past" seems almost to be a warm-up exercise for her second novel, *Treasures of Time.* Like the latter, it uses an archaeological motif to explore the difficulty people have with seeing the past clearly. The protagonist, a university student named Susan, spends the summer volunteering on an archaeological dig, mainly to help her get her mind off a recent unhappy love affair. In the course of this therapeutic summer, she discovers a sincere interest in archaeology—suddenly realizing, as did the young Penelope Lively, that the past is real—and Lively subtly interweaves the girl's struggles to understand the historical past with her struggles to see her personal past more clearly.

Another story that strikes one as a warm-up exercise for a particular novel is "The Art of Biography," first published in 1981. Like *According to Mark*, which appeared three years later, this story portrays a scholar who is writing the biography of a deceased literary man and who in the course of his research encounters myriad, conflicting views of his subject. In almost mystery tale fashion, Malcolm, like Mark, tries to piece together these diverse accounts and ultimately arrives at the insight that there is no definitive version of a person's life.

This assertion of the subjective nature of reality, which of course is a major feature of Lively's novels, is expressed in a number of additional stories. In "Corruption," for example, a staid middle-aged couple—a judge and his magistrate wife—go off for a working holiday weekend, bringing along material concerning the pornography case they are currently involved in. Staying at their hotel is an attractive divorcée who Richard believes is making sexual overtures toward him. Regarding himself as a moral person, he coolly rebuffs her. Later when he and his wife are sitting on the beach doing some paperwork, the stack of case-related pornographic magazines they have brought along is suddenly scattered all over the beach by a strong wind. The divorcée, sitting nearby, gathers up a bunch and, no doubt assuming the couple are perusing the magazines for salacious reasons, returns them to the judge with the contemptuous comment, "people are not what they seem to be."[18] Lively seems here to be making her characteristic point that one's interpretation of reality depends on one's angle of vision. The story ends with the suggestion that the judge's impression of the divorcée is probably as subjective and squinting as is hers of him.

In a few stories Lively expresses the same fascination with time and the workings of memory that she displays extensively in her novels. "Venice, Now and Then" demonstrates the intricate way our memories are interwoven with our consciousness of the present. Third-person objective reportage of a conversation between two people is interspersed with first-person, present-tense flashbacks to an earlier experience they shared. As in the novels, this technique allows Lively to reveal that the past continually recurs in our consciousness, that our memory of an event is continually revised in light of subsequent events, and that no two people experience the same event in the same way.

In addition to the types of stories discussed thus far—those linked closely to the author's personal experience and those concerned with the major themes of her novels—Lively's oeuvre contains a third category of short stories: sharp social satires. In only one novel, *Next to Nature, Art,* does Lively give full rein to her satirical streak, but it is expressed extensively in many short stories. These are crisp little pieces in which the satire comes across in good part through dialogue and action, with very little authorial intrusion, much the same way that it does in *Next to Nature, Art.* The target of the satire is usually social, intellectual, or artistic pretentiousness.

A deftly ironic tale entitled "Servants Talk about People: Gentlefolk Discuss Things" exposes the hypocrisy of an upper-class couple who pretend to be interested in ideas and politics but whose talk reveals them to be preoccupied with social rank and physical appearance. Taking their graduate student nephew, Tim, out to lunch at an upscale restaurant, Lucy and Rupert feign an interest in his academic work and his political involvement but then constantly interrupt him to swerve the conversation back to their own shallow concerns. Lively's satiric bite and her flair for dramatic irony are brilliantly displayed here, especially when she shows that Lucy and Rupert, who claim to be very "people-oriented," are totally oblivious to the feelings and even the sex of the waitress: to the suppressed irritation of their more sensitive nephew, they keep referring to her as the "waiter" and don't even notice that she is painfully upset about something.

A similar story, "Pack of Cards," contrasts the liberal, intellectual values of a likable young man with the pretentious, shallow ones of the upper-class people he associates with. The protagonist, Nick, attends a luncheon with his girlfriend, Charlotte, at the estate of her wealthy matriarch grandmother, an imperious old woman who prides herself on her literary connections and her extensive library. During the course of the visit, however, it becomes increasingly apparent that no one in the family has actually read any of the books in the much-touted collection and that they're merely a showpiece. In the wonderfully amusing and ironic climax to the story, Nick takes down a book to read and is met with astonishment and annoyance by the rest of the party. Having finally had enough of their hypocrisy, he utters with contempt that "it's high time someone read these books" and marches out of the house, flinging back at their incredulous faces, à la Alice, "You're nothing but a pack of cards!"[19]

Academic types are occasionally the target of Lively's satire. "Presents of Fish and Game" portrays a college committee discussing candidates for a fellowship in modern history. As the meeting proceeds, the new junior fellow becomes disillusioned to discover that the older professors are motivated not by scholarly concerns but by self-interest and insecurity about their own status. In the grotesque satire "Revenant as Typewriter" a rigid professor who prides herself on her refined academic tastes and considers herself totally in control of her life begins increasingly and uncontrollably to behave like the sexy, philistine woman who used to own her house. The story is reminiscent of the children's novels *The Ghost of Thomas Kempe* and *The Revenge of Samuel Stokes* in the way the "ghost" of the previous inhabitant noisily reasserts herself, but its main effect is a satiric lancing of the academic's smugness.

In a few stories the satire involves a clash between old and young. "Miss Carlton and the Pop Concert" is a sharply ironic piece in which an open-minded old woman attends a rock concert in Hyde Park and seats herself among a group of artsy-looking young people. Attracted by their appearance, which puts her in mind of the bohemian art students of her own day, she attempts to engage them in meaningful conversation but is disappointed to discover that beneath the unconventional-looking garb reside highly conventional, bourgeois attitudes.

"Party" contrasts the decency and morality of an elderly woman with the self-centeredness and hedonism of the younger generations of her family. During Ellen Greaves's visit at the London home of her daughter and son-in-law, they throw a party for their own middle-aged friends and for their teenaged children's friends. As the occasion degenerates into decadence and bacchanalia, with the older generation drinking too much and flirting with each other's spouses and the younger generation smoking marijuana, necking, and passing out on sofas and beds, only Ellen maintains decorum and tries to make authentic conversation. Finally, in the wee hours of the morning, she ascends to the bedroom where her youngest grandchild, 11-year-old Paul, has been secluding himself all evening, and the two of them have a truly festive "party" that contrasts sharply with the stygian goings-on downstairs. In quiet, affectionate companionship they collaborate on assembling a tricky model airplane, and when finished celebrate by drinking a cup of cocoa together. With a deft touch, Lively has here portrayed the same kind of empathetic grandparent-grandchild relationship that figures in so many of her children's novels.

The pieces in Lively's final category of stories are concerned with eccentrics and bear a certain resemblance to the cartoonlike tales of James Thurber. Although in her novels Lively includes a few peripheral oddball characters, in a number of her stories she places such types at the center and reveals a keen eye for quirky, offbeat behavior. Many of these tales seem less serious in purpose than her others. Some are simply comical; others border on the grotesque and gothic; and a few include elements of fantasy. For example, "The Emasculation of Ted Roper" tells the story of cocky, macho, middle-aged Ted Roper whose tomcat serves as his doppelganger. The women in the village are disgusted equally by Ted's philandering and by his cat's impregnating their female cats. After some of the women capture the cat and have it secretly castrated, it becomes docile and tame, and, eerily, so does Ted.

"Black Dog" is a macabre tale, reminiscent of Thurber's "The Unicorn," about an agoraphobic woman who refuses to leave her home because she imagines she sees a threatening black dog in her yard. Despite her husband's, daughters', and psychiatrist's attempts to reason with her, she persists in her delusion, even putting out a bowl of dog food to placate the dog. "Customers" is an amusing tale about a pair of loony con artists, Major Anglesey and his mistress, Mrs. Yardley-Peters. The two spend their days pulling off masterful shoplifting jobs, only to go home and stash the goods in a closet with apparently no intention of using them or selling them. The story ends with their ritualistic celebration of the day's success: an absurd Alice-in-Wonderland type of tea party in which they eat off of Beatrix Potter play china and speak baby-talk to each other.

Lively's body of short fiction, then, comprises a variety of types of stories. These include the offbeat and macabre; the sharply satirical; those that touch on the themes about time, memory, and subjectivity that figure extensively in her novels; and those that capture experiences and emotions from her own past. But as disparate as they are in subject and mood, all her stories are characterized by the same conciseness and understatedness, traits that have drawn wide praise from reviewers and caused them to liken Lively's stories to those of Chekhov and Joyce as well as to the spare modern-day *New Yorker* story.

Chapter Two

The Road to Lichfield and *Treasures of Time*

Although Penelope Lively rightly rejects the notion held by some that the writing of children's fiction is merely an apprenticeship for the writing of adult fiction (Hardyment, 31), in a sense this can be said to have been true of her own experience. Her first two adult novels, *The Road to Lichfield* (1977) and *Treasures of Time* (1979), written after she had published at least eight children's novels, are notably polished, with none of the awkwardness or tentativeness of theme or technique one sometimes finds in an author's early efforts. On the contrary, her style is poised and sure, and her themes reflect years of germination in her juvenile fiction. There seems to have been a natural evolution from the literal ghosts and time warps of her children's novels to the ghosts of memory and history and the exploration of psychological time that figure in her adult novels.

The Road to Lichfield

It is easy to account for the initial and continued popularity of *The Road to Lichfield,* shortlisted for the 1977 Booker Prize. Written in the appealingly self-possessed, witty manner that has come to characterize the author's prose style, it portrays the kind of ordinary, constrained lives most of us lead but infuses these portraits with broad authorial sympathy, insight, and humor. Furthermore, it contains intelligent, likable characters, presented in depth, whom most readers can readily relate to.

The Plot and the Novel's Appeal

The plot revolves around Anne Linton, a 40-year-old housewife and part-time history teacher living in the Berkshire suburb of Cuxing. Anne is the prototype of many of Lively's later female protagonists: astute and intellectual, but more involved with family, household, and community concerns than with her career. The action takes place over the course of a spring and summer when Anne's widowed father, James Stanway, is dying in a nursing home in Lichfield. His precarious condition necessitates Anne's making several trips to Lichfield to visit him and to straighten out his house and his affairs. In the course of these visits, a number of psychologically disorienting events occur that cause Anne to readjust her views of her father, her life, and her marriage.

In the process of sorting through her father's papers and bank statements, Anne gradually begins to suspect a disquieting truth, which is finally confirmed by her older brother, Graham: her father, who had lived an apparently quiet, respectable life as a family man and a school inspector, had for years carried on a clandestine extramarital affair with a divorcée and had contributed to the support of the woman's daughter. This information jolts Anne, for it alters her understanding not only of her father but also of her parents' relationship and of her entire childhood. At the same time that she is making this discovery about her father, she is making an equally disorienting one about herself. In a pattern uncannily similar to her father's, she too becomes involved in a serious extramarital affair and begins to lead a double life.

Although her marriage of 17 years has been seemingly untroubled and monogamous, it is clear that there are dissatisfactions Anne has not allowed herself to admit. In fact, the only weak aspect of this novel is Lively's portrait of the marriage: it is hard to believe that Anne, who we learn from flashbacks and from other characters' thoughts was a passionate, talkative young woman, would have chosen to marry a cold and taciturn person like Don Linton, whose only interest seems to be getting ahead in his legal career and moving to a more posh house. But the marriage, anchored by two children, has worked well enough and Anne has squelched her disappointment. This changes, however, when she meets her father's former neighbor, 42-year-old David Fielding, headmaster and history teacher at a boys' school near Lichfield and, like Anne, living with a less than satisfying marriage.

David and Anne, who discover their mutual interest in history, strike up a companionable relationship during the course of Anne's visits, sharing dinners at a local pub and chatting over cups of tea in her father's kitchen. But there is also a sexual attraction that becomes increasingly difficult for them to ignore and to which they finally succumb. For the next few months Anne lives a dazed, divided existence, experiencing simultaneously the heady euphoria of romantic love and the debilitating guilt of infidelity.

The affair is finally concluded when the respective spouses learn of it and indicate that they will not make an issue of it if it is quietly terminated. Neither Anne nor David being by nature rash enough to fly in the face of convention and break up their families, they comply with their spouses' wishes. This ending no doubt disappoints readers of a romantic inclination and irritates feminist readers who would prefer that Anne liberate herself from a conventional, stultifying marriage. But it rings true to many others, who recognize that most lives are in fact subject to such compromises. Indeed, one of the novel's greatest strengths is its sympathetic and realistic portrayal of the way people struggle with life's limitations. This theme is conveyed not only through the situations of Anne and David but also through those of secondary characters, such as James Stanway, who is astonished by the physical and mental decline of old age, and Anne's brother, Graham, who is experiencing the midlife realization that his choice of a fast-track life-style, so glamorous in his 20s, has left him a lonely bachelor. Even Anne's husband, Don, the only really unlikable character in the book, receives our sympathy when, suddenly realizing that he has fewer career years ahead of him than behind, he is filled with an uncomfortable awareness of the inexorable nature of time.

Another reason for the novel's appeal is its social realism and satire. Lively creates a subplot that allows her to portray the superficiality and shallowness characteristic of the suburban gentry class to which Anne, because of her husband's profession, belongs. At the request of a neighbor named Sandra Butterfield, a wonderfully sketched stereotype of the well-heeled socially minded matron who seeks out causes "with the fervour of a medieval churchman in pursuit of a heresy,"[1] Anne agrees to become involved with the Splatt's Cottage Preservation Committee. This is a group of civic-minded villagers who militate against the destruction of an ancient local cottage by a housing developer. In some sharply satirical scenes Lively expresses her scorn for those who get caught up in historical preservation solely because it has become fashionable. For example, at a committee meeting held at the stylishly rustic home of two of the members, Mary and Brian Pickering, Anne, who has a genuine interest in history, notes with irritation that the Pickerings have displayed historical artifacts and tools as decorations on their rough-hewn walls. The hollowness of the couple's appreciation of history is revealed when, in answer to one of the guests' questions, they indicate that they don't even know the original functions of these items.

In satiric scenes such as the above, Lively reveals her skill at depicting social situations. She is equally skilled at psychological verisimilitude. She frequently portrays the way consciousness and perception operate, in particular the way sensory impressions of peripheral events interact with thoughts and emotions, especially in situations of anxiety. This can be seen in the episode when Graham confirms Anne's growing but unarticulated suspicion that their father had a mistress. Although narrated in the third person, the point of view is primarily Anne's:

> Graham put his glass down. He swirled its base in the circle of damp it had left on the table. Outside in the kitchen, coke cascaded into the boiler. Graham took a handkerchief from his pocket and wiped the wet patch and the base of the glass. He put the handkerchief away and the glass down and said, "Yes. The fact is. . . . Look, Anne, I always imagined you had some idea."
>
> "Some idea of what?" More coke pouring. Diffused spatter of an overspill.
>
> "Well, clearly you didn't. Look, Annie, you aren't going to like this, but the fact is Dad had a lady off-stage for a long time. In Gloucester or some such place."
>
> The lid of the boiler clunked shut. The hod was dumped down on the floor. Now Don was washing his hands.
>
> Anne said, "You cannot, you simply cannot be telling me he had a mistress." (*RL*, 52)

This scene aptly captures the way minor events going on around us register with greater sharpness when we are wrought up emotionally.

It is the novel's psychological and social precision, then, along with its sympathetic characters and its focus on the perennially interesting topics of marriage and aging, that accounts for its widespread appeal. But the novel is more than the sensitive, entertaining piece of realism the above plot summary may suggest. It is also, as the ensuing analysis will show, an exploration of complex epistemological issues concerned with the relationship between human consciousness and history, time, and reality.

History

Although Lively chose to make her career as novelist rather than historian, it was her reading of history at the university that determined the kind of fiction she would write, as she herself has acknowledged (Hardyment, 30). And, indeed, she uses her fiction to air her passionate, polemical views on this subject. In her first two novels the main characters—Anne and David in *The Road to Lichfield* and Tom Rider in *Treasures of Time*—are historians who give voice to many of her own ideas.

Like her author, Anne Linton is acutely sensitive to historical vestiges in the landscape. Driving the road to Lichfield, she cannot view with an innocent eye the villages and fields she passes through but instead sees them steeped in their historical associations, "the landscape itself a palimpsest, suggesting another time, another place. Edgehill recalled the Civil War; Tamworth, lurking over to the right, had something Saxon about it, she seemed to remember" (*RL,* 1). Lively, of course, has this same sensibility, as she reveals at length in her book about landscape history, *The Presence of the Past.*

Author and character also share a passion for exploring ancient cathedrals and archaeological sites. For them this is more than the fashionable hobby it is for many people; rather, it grows out of a deep-seated fascination and curiosity concerning older cultures. An episode in the novel that reveals this attitude is Anne and Don's visit to a neolithic burial ground: whereas Don merely goes through the motions, Anne deeply engages with the activity, musing, "You can't begin to imagine what they were feeling, those people, trailing up here burying each other with pots and brooches and goodness knows what" (*RL,* 75).

It is this awareness of the difficulty of truly understanding the past that is at the root of Anne's interest in history. Like Lively, she believes that one of the reasons people cannot see the past clearly is that they've been influenced by the contemporary tendency to regard it as quaint, thereby distorting and diminishing it—or, as Lively has said, "treating the past as entertainment."[2] One of the major targets of her criticism is the television industry's production of slick historical costume dramas, which contribute to the public's view of the past as picturesque. In *The Road to Lichfield* Anne's media mogul brother glibly describes to her the eight-episode "historical soap-opera" (*RL,* 198) about Sir Walter Raleigh he is producing: the Tower of London is "just handy as a central theme— you know, take something solid like a place and watch history seething around it and all that, it's a good device, gives us scope to bring in just about everything. Good old bread-and-butter costume drama, everybody loves it" (*RL,* 198). Viewing the filming of one of these episodes, Anne witnesses the absurdity and superficiality of this approach: the directors and camera crew are focused more on image than substance, and their jargon-laden commands continually interrupt the actors' dialogue. Anne's skepticism of this approach to history reflects Lively's.

Another major target of Lively's criticism is the popular taste for antiques and historical artifacts. Anne's clever teenaged son, Paul, sums up this attitude when he points out that "it's posh to like old things. . . . Antique furniture and houses with beams everywhere, and vintage cars. And old maps. Dead posh. It shows you've got nice taste" (*RL,* 57).

Anne is equally cynical, as witnessed in her reaction, discussed earlier, to the antique tools decorating the Pickerings' home. What bothers her about this fad is that it contributes to the contemporary tendency to diminish the past: "Each object was wrenched from its own past. It was as though by displaying what had gone before and making an ornament of it, you destroyed its potency. Less sophisticated societies propitiate their ancestors; this one makes a display of them and renders them harmless" (*RL,* 178).

Anne's unfashionable beliefs about history frequently land her in difficult situations. She loses her job because she insists on teaching children about "what actually happened" (*RL,* 188) rather than presenting history "in nice digestible chunks, as themes or projects" (*RL,* 188). And she is asked to step down as secretary of the Splatt's Cottage Preservation Committee because she questions the wisdom of preservation at all costs.

This subplot about Splatt's Cottage allows Lively to give full expression to her criticism of contemporary attitudes toward the past. Although Anne's instinctive appreciation of old buildings inclines her to take an interest in the Splatt's Cottage cause, she is also skeptical of the fashionable tendency to "sanctify the past just for its own sake" (*RL,* 47). Visiting the cottage and noting the terribly dilapidated shape it's in, she reflects wryly, "Extraordinary, really—you take a tree and chop it in half and build a house out of it, and people come along, hundreds of years later, and stick iron ranges into it made in Birmingham and glass lamp-shades from Woolworth's. And somewhere along the line there is some curious adjustment to the way people feel about the past and it becomes immoral to knock the place down" (*RL,* 41).

Her skepticism increases when she interviews Mr. Jewkes, the planning officer, and realizes that his argument for the benefits of demolishing the cottage to replace it with low-cost housing for the elderly is much better thought out than the simplistic, emotional argument of the preservation committee. Anne finds herself agreeing with this man, whose words about the importance of a healthy mixture of old and new seem to come directly from the author's mouth. Anne's speech on resigning from the committee also seems a straightforward expression of Lively's sentiments: "It's just I feel worried about indiscriminate hanging onto the past—in the form of buildings, or—or anything else. Sometimes I think we're not too sure why we're doing it—and we may not even be quite clear what it is we're hanging onto. But at the same time I think it's very important to know about it—but to know proper ly, not just to have a vague idea or even to adapt it to suit your own purposes" (*RL*, 189).

Anne's—and Lively's—view that people tend to romanticize the past is vindicated when the bulldozer demolishing the cottage unearths some skeletons of children buried outside the kitchen door. Autopsies reveal that they had apparently starved to death during the early nineteenth century, when the price of corn was so high that many people couldn't afford to feed their offspring. This discovery supports Anne's point by exposing the very unromantic reality of the cottage's history.

Memory

Not only the historical but also the personal past is of consuming interest to Lively. She is fascinated by the intricate interplay between memory and consciousness, believing that people, like places, have a "palimpsest quality" and are made up of "layerings of memory" ("Bones," 644). In her forays into the thought processes of the novel's main characters, she demonstrates the way our pasts are ever-present in our minds. Indeed, much of the artistic coherence of this novel derives from Lively's skillful counterpointing of events in the present with recurring flashbacks to events in the past that many of the main characters experienced in common.

One of these recollections is of a family seaside vacation at Southwold, taken when Anne and Graham were children. The memory is first conjured up when old Mr. Stanway mistakenly hears Anne say "Southwold" instead of "Scotland" in her description of a holiday she and Don are planning:

> "Southwold," the old man said, with sudden clarity.
>
> "Not Southwold, Scotland."
>
> "We took you to Southwold when you were a child, your mother and I."
>
> "Southwold in Suffolk? Yes, I remember."
>
> "You remember?" He seemed pleased.
>
> "You bought me a red spade. And there were sea-birds running in and out of the water at low tide—I can see them now. Little spindly legs skittering about." (*RL*, 6)

As Anne relives this memory, past and present seem to merge, and she experiences a kind of double-vision of her father. She gazes at his decrepit body in the nursing home bed but simultaneously sees "that same body, upright in a pewter sea [at Southwold], urging her towards it with outstretched hands" (*RL,* 7). Several pages later Graham, in his London apartment, gazes out into the night at the lights of a traffic jam and is "reminded . . . unaccountably, of a fun-fair. Once long ago, he had ridden on a dodgem or some such thing at a fun-fair and red lights had glittered, thus, against a backdrop of water, as, now, the Thames shone black beyond the Embankment. . . . He was nagged, irritatingly, by this fitful memory until all of a sudden it clarified itself. In Southwold, once, on holiday when he and Anne were kids, there had been such a fun-fair on the promenade; the lights, the sea. Christ, he thought, whatever brought that back?" (*RL,* 16).

Often it is places rich in personal associations that trigger Proustian plunges into the past for Lively's characters. This is particularly true for Anne, who, sharing the author's sensibility, believes that "places aren't quite as detached as they're made out to be" (*RL,* 196). For example, an impulsive sentimental visit she pays to the street in Oxford where Don resided when she first fell in love with him causes her to reexperience in vivid detail those long-ago emotions. And of course the road to Lichfield itself, which Anne has traveled so many times over the years, is rich with memories. Indeed, she sometimes feels while driving it "as though the sequence of her own life had been tampered with, as though she were again the young woman who used to come up here to visit her parents. The edge of her own face in the driving mirror, eye and swatch of hair, was not, fleetingly seen, so very different after all from the face of twenty years ago" (*RL,* 11).

Lively believes that memories are an essential part of our individual and collective identity,[3] but she is also aware of how subjective and tenuous memories are. A major theme of this book is the difficulty of viewing the past clearly. Whereas the subplot, as we have seen, explores the way we distort the historical past, the main plot does the same for the personal past. Anne's trips to Lichfield over the course of the summer really constitute a journey into her own past, for the process of cleaning out her father's house and going through old family papers, letters, and photograph albums stirs up numerous childhood memories. But the jolting discoveries she makes about her father over the course of this summer cause her to realize that she has not had an objective or complete grasp of the past, for "things that appeared so, were not" (*RL,* 54).

Whereas Anne recalls her father as a quiet man whose primary identity lay in his family role, she begins to discover that he appeared very differently to others: as talkative and outgoing to his mistress's daughter, as "a bachelor type" (*RL,* 19) to his housekeeper, and—what is suggested by a collection of his earnestly penned professional correspondence that Anne unearths—as a committed educator to his colleagues. She must therefore readjust her memories to accommodate these new views of him. Looking at old photographs of family outings, she realizes now what a false picture of family togetherness they present, for her father's mistress "must have loomed large behind all these snaps" (*RL,* 91).

Anne becomes bemused by the idea that we inevitably distort the past, both public and private. And so she is intrigued when she and David discover that a Latvian immigrant they have recently met who described to them his idyllic, prosperous childhood was in fact not recalling things accurately. She says to David, "I suppose that's what we do. Not so much preserve things as distort them" (*RL,* 118) and then muses to herself about the universality of this phenomenon: "A middle-aged Latvian long resident in Staffordshire remembers a farmhouse that possibly never was; I knew my father in one dimension only; in Cuxing people are prepared to go to surprising lengths to keep other people from knocking down a building that can never have been so valued before" (*RL,* 118).

Subjectivity and Lively's Narrative Technique

Anne's heightened awareness of the difficulty of viewing the past objectively reflects the author's own preoccupation with the subjectiveness of all our perceptions, not just our pictures of the past. In both fiction and nonfiction Lively has expressed her interest in the question of the tenuous nature of the evidence on which we build our knowledge of the world.[4] Early in *The Road to Lichfield* she addresses this topic when she has Anne, who is sifting through her father's papers and memorabilia, muse that "this random archive of paper in his desk was the same kind of fitful evidence about people's lives as those miraculously surviving scraps of Saxon writs and medieval tax returns" she had once come across while working in the manuscript room of a museum. "They told you facts, but facts stripped of the whole truth. She looked at her wedding photos and thought: mother looks glum but in fact she was the only one who really enjoyed it" (*RL,* 23–24).

In this novel Lively introduces the narrative technique, which she claims to have derived from the Japanese film *Rashomon* ("Fiction and

Reality," 21), that she will use in much of her later fiction to demon-strate the partial nature of evidence and the squinting way individuals perceive reality. Employing a shifting (among the main characters) third-person limited point of view throughout the novel, she occasion-ally presents the same episode two or more times, each time from the vantage point of a different participant. For example, a visit to Coventry cathedral by Anne, Graham, and their father in the early years of Anne's marriage is recalled differently by each of the partici-pants, underscoring the discrepancies between their perceptions. Whereas Anne was interpreting her father's argumentative mood that day as mere crankiness, he was actually trying to engage her in spirited debate to revive her old self, which he feared was being squelched by her dull husband. And whereas she assumed that Graham, newly launched in his glamorous television career, was intensely bored with the provincial outing, his aloofness was really caused by his preoccupa-tion with thoughts about the girl he had just fallen in love with and was considering marrying. No single version of this event, then, is "true" or complete.

Assessment of Lively's First Novel

The use of the kaleidoscopic method in *The Road to Lichfield* adumbrates what has become Lively's characteristic narrative technique, employed to its most dazzling effect in her seventh novel, *Moon Tiger*. Her first novel also introduces the concerns with history, memory, and subjectivity that have proven to be the sustaining themes of Lively's adult fiction.

But *The Road to Lichfield* is more than merely a precursor to the author's later work; it is also a strong piece of fiction in its own right, remarkably smooth and subtle for a first novel. It is to Lively's credit as an artist that she is able to create a highly patterned novel (there are par-allels, for example, between various characters' lives, such as Anne's and her father's, as well as between the complexity of Anne's personal past and that of the historical past; likewise, the journey to Lichfield is both a geographical and a psychological journey into Anne's past[5]) without becoming heavy-handed and obvious. This is because the novel's pat-terning and scaffolding never take precedence over its "felt life" quality. What readers are most aware of when absorbed in *The Road to Lichfield* is the "rightness" of the author's portrayal of the small, ordinary moments of existence: a mother's mixture of pity and irritation when dealing with her taciturn teenaged daughter; the phenomenon of making perfunctory small talk at a party while simultaneously thinking about more burning, personal concerns; the painful awkwardness of trying to carry on a conversation with one's elderly, senile parent. It is in the precise rendering of common human experiences such as these that Lively's novelistic strengths are most fully displayed.

Treasures of Time

Lively's second adult novel, *Treasures of Time,* is as polished as her first and contains many of the same ingredients: a cluster of interesting, mostly likable characters whose different consciousnesses are explored in depth; a crisp, concise style; a number of deftly satiric scenes; and a focus on the way the past, both historical and personal, is intricately involved with the present. Like *The Road to Lichfield,* this novel was well received, winning the Arts Council National Book Award and being praised by reviewers for its subtle and graceful style, its realistic portrayal of character and place, and its coherent weaving of the theme of the past into all aspects of the narrative.

In many ways, though, it is a more accomplished work than *The Road to Lichfield.* Whereas in writing that book Lively had merely to rely on her firsthand familiarity with middle-class suburban life, for this book she had to research the unfamiliar field of archaeology, with which much of the plot is concerned. She also set herself the task of creating a protagonist very unlike herself—a young man of 25 from a working-class background. Lively proved to be successful at both these endeavors. Tom Rider, the protagonist, is a fully realized, believable character, and the eminent archaeologist Stewart Piggott said of *Treasures of Time,* "Archaeologically, I cannot fault it."[6]

The novel is also technically more sophisticated than *The Road to Lichfield.* The kaleidoscopic narrative method she experimented with in that book is here used more extensively and skillfully, and the floating third-person narrator dips in and out of the consciousnesses of a larger, more diverse range of characters, including those of a 6-year-old child and a 60-year-old stroke victim. Because she renders each character's consciousness in a distinctly different voice, Lively is able to report the same episode several times without seeming monotonous or repetitive. On the contrary, with each turn of the kaleidoscope she deepens our understanding of the complexity of human responses to the world and of the tenuousness of reality.

The Plot

At the center of the novel is likable, frankly spoken Tom Rider, a graduate of Oxford who is working on his doctoral thesis in history and scrap-
ing by on a meager national grant. He spends his days at the British
Museum researching the life of his thesis subject, William Stukeley, an
eighteenth-century antiquarian. Tom has recently become engaged to and
moved into a flat with Kate Paxton, the 24-year-old daughter of the late
Hugh Paxton, a celebrated archaeologist whose excavation of a neolithic
burial site in Wiltshire was a major breakthrough in the archaeological
understanding of prehistoric British culture. Kate, who inherited her
father's interest in archaeology, works as a civil servant setting up museum exhibits of artifacts from different periods of Britain's past.

Tom and Kate are in many ways an incongruous couple: sociable and
talkative, he likes nothing better than to sit late in a pub arguing with
cronies, whereas Kate is tense, awkward, and jealous and would prefer to
spend her evenings alone with a book or with Tom. Kate attributes her
personality difficulties to her mother, and when Tom finally meets the
latter, toward the beginning of the novel, he cannot help but agree.

Laura Paxton, beautiful and socially polished, presides over the family's rural Wiltshire estate, Danehurst, now gone somewhat to seed
owing to Laura's financial ineptness. Sharing the house with her is her
older maiden sister, Nellie, a recent stroke victim, who, having managed
her money better, contributes financial help in return for Laura's physical assistance. On his first weekend visit to Danehurst, Tom immediately sizes up Laura: he recognizes that she is one of those self-centered,
superficial people who take pleasure in putting everyone else at a disad-
vantage. He now understands how Kate, who as a no doubt clumsy,
plain-looking child was a disappointment to her appearance-conscious
mother, has been affected by Laura.

Much of the novel takes place at Danehurst, and via flashbacks and
exposure to the private thoughts of Laura, Nellie, and Kate we learn a
great deal about relations among the Paxton family members, both living and deceased. It is revealed that Nellie, herself an archaeologist and a
long-term colleague of Hugh's, for years harbored a powerful, secret love
for this man, who against his better judgment fell prey to the physical
charms of her shallow younger sister. The marriage was fraught with difficulties, caused in part by Laura's predilection for infidelities—one of
which traumatized six-year-old Kate when she discovered it—and by
Laura's jealousy of the close friendship between Hugh and Nellie.

Lively does a masterful job of characterizing these two women. Nellie is a familiar type in Lively's fiction—the intelligent, wry, no-nonsense older woman—but in this work the author has set herself the challenge of adding a physical handicap to the character. Never descending into pathos, Lively manages to create a realistic portrayal of the frustrations such a person experiences. Reviewer Susan Hill puts it well when she states that "the portrait of Nellie is the most acute, shrewd and compassionate one of a person with a handicap and affliction, I have read for many a year. How Nellie's thoughts, observations, emotions, memories, exist like an absolutely clear, flowing stream, below the flat rock which has shut down upon her, trapping her in slow, blurred speech and paralysed movement, is most beautifully conveyed."[7]

Laura, too, is a familiar type in Lively's fiction, particularly in her satirical short stories: the superficial society matron who is preoccupied with appearance and status. But as she does with Nellie, Lively sets herself the challenge of adding something to this characterization: she actually makes Laura somewhat sympathetic by probing the recesses of her consciousness and thereby revealing Laura's deep, neurotic insecurities and sense of shame. For the most part, however, Lively has a great deal of fun exposing Laura's pretentiousness in the kind of satirical comedy-of-manners scenes the author is so good at. Particularly revealing are the conversations between Laura and her new friend, Barbara Hamilton, a woman who is almost Laura's match in social competitiveness. In one such tête-à-tête Barbara one-ups Laura's subtle name dropping with an offhand remark about her old friend "Willie Maugham," whom she'd known "rather well," causing Laura to seethe to herself, "One slightly tiresome thing about Barbara was the way she would keep mentioning important or interesting people she knew or had known, who were often as, if not more, important and interesting than the people one knew or had known oneself" (*TT,* 61).

The Paxton family and their relationships thus constitute one focus of the novel. But more central to the novel is Tom Rider and his relationships, especially his involvement with Kate. This gradually deteriorates as he becomes increasingly irritated by her personality problems. These are highlighted when she accompanies Tom on a weekend visit to the country cottage of his old friends Martin and Beth Laker, an endearing young couple with three small children who have chosen to live a counterculture, back-to-the-earth life-style. Kate feels threatened by the easygoing, open manners of the Lakers and reacts by becoming even stiffer than usual. A few weeks later when she and Tom run into Martin's comely sister, Cherry, with whom Tom once had an affair, Kate becomes jealous, jumping to the conclusion that Tom had secretly planned the meeting. In fact Tom had harbored no such intentions, but in exasperation with Kate he goes off to have lunch at a pub with Cherry and, his penchant for drink and his youthful randiness getting the best of him, ends up in bed with her. Although the encounter is ephemeral and Tom ultimately confesses to Kate and patches things up, the relationship never quite regains its old footing. One senses that on some level Tom is beginning to realize that women like Cherry—warm, expansive, and talkative—are more suited to him than the prickly Kate. Ultimately he does break off the engagement.

In addition to worrying about his relationship with Kate, Tom spends much of his time ruminating about his thesis and his career prospects. Lively knows the academic life well, and her presentation of the process of researching and writing a thesis is realistic. Tom spends a great deal of his time trying to imagine how the world appeared to William Stukeley, thus revealing Lively's understanding of the way one can become completely absorbed by a subject. He is also beset from time to time by the usual graduate student doubts about the significance of his topic and about the wisdom of pursuing a career with dim job prospects. Tom, in short, is a well-drawn character who rings particularly true to academic readers.

Another major line of interest in the novel is the making of a television documentary about Hugh Paxton's career. During Tom and Kate's first weekend visit at Danehurst, Laura announces that she has been contacted by a fellow at the BBC who wants to do such a program. Kate and Nellie, repulsed by the idea of commercializing serious work, express their antipathy for the project, but flashy Laura is all for it and has her way. Over the remainder of the summer the BBC producer, Tony Greenway, and his crew spend a great deal of time at Danehurst and at nearby Charlie's Tump, the site of the famous excavation. Hugh's career is a frequent topic of conversation among all the characters, and here Lively reveals her grasp of both the technical aspects of archaeology— the digs and the cataloguing of findings—and the history of archaeological theories and movements. Tom is particularly intrigued by the subject because there are parallels between Paxton's work and that of Tom's man Stukeley, who conducted archaeological explorations in this same area two and a half centuries earlier. It is in fact Tom who inadvertently supplies the title for the documentary, "Treasures of Time," when he remarks to Tony Greenway that Charlie's Tump puts him in mind of a sentence in Sir Thomas Browne's seventeenth-century work *Urn Burial:* "The treasures of time lie high, in Urnes, Coynes, and Monuments, scarce below the roots of some vegetables" (*TT,* 55).[8]

The actual filming of the documentary, toward the end of the book, is the novel's climactic episode. With everyone gathered at Danehurst, most of the plot lines are resolved: the film is completed; Tom and Kate finally break up; and Nellie suddenly dies, triggering in Laura, it appears, a recognition of her deep attachment to her sister buried under all the jealousy, and thus in a sense resolving their relationship. The only plot line not resolved during this penultimate chapter—the question of Tom's career—is dealt with in the final one. His thesis completed but no academic job prospects in sight, Tom decides to accept Tony Greenway's offer to work as his research assistant for BBC historical programs. The novel concludes in an open-ended fashion, with Tom traveling on the train to London and his unknown future, feeling ambivalent but excited.

Uses and Abuses of the Past

A major theme of this novel is the subjective and culturally conditioned way we view the historical past. Most of the characters, living as well as deceased, have both shaped and been shaped by their era's interpretation of the past: Tom is a historian writing his thesis on an eighteenth-century antiquarian who himself studied ancient cultures; Kate creates museum exhibits of historical periods; Hugh Paxton was an archaeologist, as is Aunt Nellie; and Tony Greenway produces television documentaries about historical figures and events. The cast of characters thus gives Lively wide scope to explore this topic that is of perpetual interest to her.

Like *The Road to Lichfield*'s Anne Linton, Tom Rider shares many of the author's views about history. He is aware that the distant past is not real to most people, and he believes it is the job of historians and antiquarians to try to make it real, as did William Stukeley in the early stage of his career when he "stumped around the Wiltshire downs, measuring lumps and bumps in the turf and doing his bit to free the landscape of fantasy" (*TT,* 46). As a child Tom experienced the same quasimystical insight into the reality of history that the adolescent Lively did: on an outing to a stately home, while gazing at the portrait of a seventeenth-century gentleman posed beside a fireplace, he learned from the tour guide that that fireplace was the very same one in front of which the tour group now stood, and "Tom, confronted with this simple piece of information, this juxtaposition of the vanished and the extant, had looked at the strong-featured face in the portrait and seen, suddenly, a real man, albeit no longer here but nonetheless real for that. The past, he had realized, is true" (*TT,* 43).

This experience caused Tom to believe that one can grasp the reality of the past by making an effort of the imagination, and it is this that he tries to do in researching his thesis subject. He attempts to look at the world through William Stukeley's eyes by immersing himself in the man's life, relishing in particular the homely and commonplace details he sometimes unearths in Stukely's diaries, such as the fact that on 4 April 1719, after a day of surveying "he had 'met with some excellent Ale'" (*TT,* 10–11). Tom feels that "it's knowing that kind of thing that makes this kind of thing [the study of a historical figure] seem slightly less of a fantasy than it does a lot of the time" (*TT,* 11). Occasionally when he is absorbed in Stukeley's diaries, chronological time seems to dissolve and Tom senses the simultaneity of the past and the present, a psychological experience many of Lively's protagonists, particularly in her children's novels, are prone to. For example, returning to his work one day after lunch, Tom "sat down again in front of his pile of books, his looseleaf files, his card-index box. Two and a half centuries away, William Stukeley, out of doors in the fresh air of May 1721, stumped around the Wiltshire downs" (*TT,* 45–46).

But at other times Tom is beset by frustration, feeling that modern men and women can never really look through the eyes of inhabitants of previous cultures. In such a mood, he reflects,

> I know a great deal about Stukeley; I probably know more about Stukeley than anybody else in the world; I know where he was on April 4, 1719, and I know who his friends were and in what language he addressed them and I know the broad course of his life from the day he was born till the day he died. The real Stukeley, of course, is effectively concealed by two hundred and fifty years of gathering confusion and conflicting interpretations of how the world may have appeared to other people. The real breathing feeling cock-and-balls prick-me-and-I-bleed Stukeley is just about as inaccessible as Neanderthal man. (*TT,* 10–11)

Tom thus shares with Lively the belief that we can never truly grasp the way people of the past experienced the world: our view is inevitably shaped by current historical theory, by cultural biases and assumptions, even by our own emotional needs. This point is borne out extensively in this novel, which explores the way professional students of the past— antiquarians, historians, archaeologists—approach their subject.

Stukeley, for example, Tom explains to a friend, examined the visible remains of cultures who had lived near Avebury and Stonehenge

> and tried to interpret them in the light of the actual historical evidence available at the time. But *then*—what's interesting is that then he was ordained, and he went off his rocker—at least went off his scientific rocker—and produced wild fantasies about the Druids. That Stonehenge was a Druidical creation and that the Druids themselves were a priestly sect who came to England from Phoenicia after the Flood and set up a kind of patriarchal religion closely allied to Christianity—in other words that they were the true ancestors of the eighteenth century Church of England. It all fitted in very nicely, you see—then you could claim the most renowned site of antiquity for the Church. (*TT,* 51)

Although Tom is critical of Stukeley's subjective interpretation of history, he is aware that pure scholarly objectivity is an impossibility. Indeed, he is influenced by the cultural biases and historical theories of his own day: in accordance with current academic fashion, which chops up history into discrete periods possessing distinct characteristics, he will argue in his thesis that Stukeley's attitudes reflect the eighteenth-century "shift from the rational to the romantic and the decline of the seventeenth century scientific approach" (*TT,* 51).

Tom is fascinated with the phenomenon whereby new historical theories evolve and influence the outlook of their times, and it occurs to him that Stukeley, Paxton, Tony Greenway, and he himself have all been involved with this process in one way or another. Just as Stukeley publicized his views and thereby revolutionized his era's ideas about Stonehenge, so Tom is "about to contribute some seventy thousand words which will analyze and pronounce upon the way in which antiquarian studies declined from the intellectual vigor of the seventeenth century into the romantic inaccuracies of the early eighteenth, with special reference to the career of William Stukeley" (*TT,* 11), thereby influencing his own era's historical views. Similarly, Hugh Paxton helped solidify and validate the emerging anti-invasionist theory of British prehistoric studies, thus unseating the earlier invasionist theory that had in its day overthrown yet an earlier theory. Tom ruminates on this phenomenon:

> The Saxons supposed the Roman towns were built by giants. Giants, gods, Druids. . . . [Historians] get it all nicely sorted out into a chronological sequence, at last—the three ages—and then along come all sorts

of disconcerting cultural overlaps that won't fit in, and cultural parallels
in the eastern Mediterranean or whatever, and they have to work out a
new explanation—the invasionist theory. And then someone dreams up
radiocarbon dating and blows everything sky high—Stonehenge far older
than Mycenae, northern megalithic tombs earlier than any other stone
buildings, and everybody has to take a deep breath and start all over
again. (*TT,* 32)

The rise and fall of historical paradigms is inevitable, of course, as Tom
well knows. But what bothers him is the conscious manipulation of these
paradigms for meretricious ends or personal gain—what Lively often
calls "cashing in on the past." Tom accuses Stukeley of "manipulating
the past for his own intellectual ends. Rather grubby intellectual ends—
shoring up the status of the C. of E." (*TT,* 51), just as he criticizes Tony
Greenway for creating television documentaries that distort and prettify
the past for a gullible public. Indeed, when Tony gets the idea to do a
program on Stukeley as part of an upcoming series, Tom notes that there
is a "parallel in Tony's instinctive need to 'use' Stukeley and the utilitar-
ianism of the early antiquaries—the determination to make intellectual,
or other capital out of our ancestors" (*TT,* 52).

But, cynic that he is, Tom is aware that all students of the past use it
to one degree or another for their own ends, himself included. Writing in
his thesis about the decline in Stukeley's scientific thinking after his ordi-
nation, he concludes, "Nevertheless . . . his early work remains as testimony to a vigorous and inquiring mind, while the pattern of his career
serves as a . . ." and then after a pause Tom cynically finishes the sentence in his mind, "useful rung for the scholarly progress of one Tom
Rider, in this present year of grace, himself involved in the same line of
business. Thus do we feed one upon another" (*TT,* 145). Even the great
Hugh Paxton, Tom believes, "like Stukeley up to a point, cashed in on
the national past, though not wittingly or with calculation, as we all do
who earn our keep at this particular trade. Stukeley, of course, distorted
in order to get the results he wanted; Hugh Paxton presumably didn't
do that. Except in the way that convenient evidence for a theory always
seems to come to hand more readily than inconvenient evidence.
Convenient Wessex man, in this case" (*TT,* 105).

Lively is thus suggesting that one's view of the past is inevitably
refracted through a number of lenses. These include self-interest as well
as the prevailing outlook of the times in which one lives. Such influences
are inescapable and Lively is therefore not arguing for an objective

approach to the past, but rather for an awareness of the forces that shape one's outlook and for the kind of healthy skepticism that Tom has.

Television and the Romanticizing of the Past

One of the most common lenses through which we look at the past is nostalgia. As has been pointed out, Lively is bemused by the popular tendency to regard the past as picturesque, which has taken the form of a mania for antiques and old-fashioned decor. In *Treasures of Time* she expresses her skepticism of this trend through Kate, who criticizes the sentimental preference for primitive kitchen devices over their more efficient modern counterparts, such as the use of beeswax rather than furniture polish and of clothes wringers rather than spin dryers. Obviously Lively, who lives in a seventeenth-century farmhouse, can understand the aesthetic attraction of things old; what disturbs her is the romantic idealizing of the past and the assumption that old is good, new is bad. The discussion Kate and Tom's friends, the Lakers, have about old-fashioned appliances reveals Lively's own belief in the importance of a healthy balance between old and new. Although the counterculture couple are prejudiced in favor of the old, they ultimately acknowledge that Kate's argument—"if everyone thought like that you wouldn't get any innovation at all" (*TT*, 91)—has some validity. But they also point out that the opposite extreme—the wholesale embrace of innovation—is just as destructive, for "getting better at things technologically doesn't always leave you better off" (*TT*, 91).

The contemporary view of the past as picturesque, of course, contributes to the unreality it has for many people. And, Lively believes, it is the popular media—advertising, magazines, and television[9]—that are in good part responsible for creating these attitudes. Particularly culpable is television, with its emphasis on image over substance and its slick, superficial treatment of historical events.

She expresses this criticism in her first novel, as we have seen, via the episode concerning Graham Stanway's production of a historical costume drama; in her second novel she does so via the plot strand concerning the television documentary about Hugh Paxton's famous excavation. As already noted, the producer of the documentary is interested in the excavation and other historical episodes only insofar as he can "use" them for his program. For example, when he and Tom visit Charlie's Tump, while the latter is being flooded with his usual insights about the mystery of the past and the difficulty of truly understanding it, Tony is strategically assessing the place with an eye for whether it will make a good filming location. When Tom utters the sentence from *Urn Burial* that he is reminded of, Tony is attracted to the surface, not the substance, of the quote. Rather than pursue the point Tom is making, he latches onto the catchy phrase "treasures of time," noting that he could use it for the title of the documentary.

The most cogent way Lively exposes the superficiality and distortion of television's treatment of historically important subjects is her presentation of the actual filming of the documentary. Declaring to himself as he is about to shoot the Charlie's Tump scene, "The joy of filming is that anything can always be made to appear otherwise," Tony goes about positioning the camera so as to rule out any ingredients in the landscape that would contradict the bucolic "uninhabited effect" he is contriving (*TT,* 193). Tom, viewing the documentary on television with his mother and father a few weeks later, notes the successfulness of Tony's endeavor: his parents buy into the illusion completely, murmuring remarks like "Lovely country" and "Look at those wild flowers" (*TT,* 214). Tom, however, reflects ironically on the realities that have been excluded: "inharmonious items like the BBC cars and the barbed-wire fence and people and dead sheep" (*TT,* 214). (One could add to this list Hugh Paxton's less than purely scholarly motive and the jealousy of some of his colleagues.) When the scene switches to Danehurst, all that Tom's parents see is an idealized, magazine-type image of country living, with lovely Laura sitting in a wicker chair and guests playing croquet on the lawn, whereas Tom knows the ugly facts the film masks: Laura's real character, the tension between himself and Kate that day, the imminent tragedy of Nellie's death, and so on.

Shots like these, along with the highly selective, edited comments by Hugh Paxton's family members and friends, create a superficial, romanticized picture of the Charlie's Tump excavation. It is this tendency of television to glamorize and distort historical events, believes Lively, that contributes to our inability to grasp the reality of the past.

"Nothing is as it seems"

Lively denounces television for consciously manipulating the public's views because human beings have a hard enough time trying to discern reality and understand history without added distortions. She believes we can never have an objective or complete understanding of events, for we are inevitably selective and subjective in the way we view evidence. In *The Road to Lichfield* Anne Linton confronts this fact when she sees how elusive is her grasp of her father's identity. In *Treasures of Time* the issue is addressed by means of the archaeology motif, with Lively showing how our understanding of the past is based on tenuous interpretations of physical evidence, interpretations that are never final or definitive.

But archaeology is just a professional, more formalized manifestation of the universal human process of trying to make sense of the events going on around us. This point is dramatically illustrated at the beginning of chapter 7, where a sequence of brief, discrete scenarios portrays three different characters sitting down separately to tackle their respective piles of evidence: Tony Greenway sits at Hugh Paxton's desk and goes through the latter's papers, attempting to build up an accurate picture of the man; at the same time "Nellie, in her room, sits, equally absorbed, before her own extracted evidence" (*TT,* 108)—Hugh's notes about the pottery findings that she intends to interpret and write an article about; and "Tom also sits at a desk," in the British Museum, and "contemplates his card-index boxes and his tidy piles of notes" about William Stukeley, the interpretation of which will result in his writing his version of Stukeley's life.

Their interpretations, however, are inevitably partial. Tony, for example, comes across a photograph of Hugh and Nellie and dismisses it as unimportant because he assumes "the sister, what is she called? her in the wheelchair" is "irrelevant" (*TT,* 108). But we readers, with a different "pile" of evidence (our knowledge of the quasiromantic relationship between Hugh and Nellie), see the photograph as significant. Lively establishes a refrain of sorts in the novel to express this point about the elusiveness of truth and the subjective, selective nature of evidence: the statement "nothing is as it seems," versions of which are uttered by various characters throughout the book.[10] And the novel is in effect a massive argument for the truth of this assertion. Lively reveals not only the collective distortions of professionals—archaeologists, historians, documentary film producers—but also the personal distortions of private individuals.

She reveals the latter in good part by using her kaleidoscopic method, retelling the most emotionally charged episodes from the various points of view of the characters involved. For example, when Kate recalls how as a girl she presented her mother, who was dressing for a luncheon engagement, with a bead necklace she'd bought, what stands out in her memory is Laura's preoccupied, dismissive response and her own bitter disappointment that her mother would not wear the gift because the colors clashed with her outfit. In Laura's version, given several pages later, many of the details about the setting and the conversation are the same but the emphasis and mood are different: Laura recalls tactfully deflecting the whiny child's inappropriate request and being motivated by the desire to help little Kate learn good taste and a sense of color. Neither Laura nor Kate, of course, is "right," for there is never a definitive interpretation of any experience.

The overall narrative structure of the novel functions to dramatize this point. Lively uses basically the same kind of shifting approach that she did in *The Road to Lichfield,* but she includes the perspectives of a larger number of characters and she jumps more rapidly from one point of view to another, with a typical chapter crisscrossing back and forth among the perspectives of four or five characters as the action unfolds. The cumulative impact of this continual shifting is a forceful impression of the incomplete nature of each character's grasp of reality.

Immersion in the Past

Lively's narrative method also involves the inclusion of numerous flashbacks. She employs these to demonstrate the extent to which people live in the past. Although as the title of a documentary "Treasures of Time" is simply a reference to the archaeological vestiges of the past that lie just beneath the earth's surface, as the title of the novel the phrase has an additional reference: the private memories that lie just beneath the surface of people's consciousnesses. And indeed, Charlie's Tump is the site of both kinds of treasures of time—the archaeological grave goods that are ties to Great Britain's historical past and the reminiscences that are ties to Kate's, Laura's, and Nellie's pasts. It is primarily through these three characters that Lively demonstrates the hold the past has on personal lives.

The first of the novel's flashbacks occurs when Kate takes Tom to see the famous excavation site during his introductory visit to Danehurst. With the same kind of susceptibility to personal ghosts lurking in the landscape that many other Lively characters have to historical ghosts, Kate is suddenly plunged into the potent childhood memory of coming across her mother committing adultery in a nearby copse while her father and Nellie and the others were involved in digging. Then at subsequent points in the novel the mention or thought of Charlie's Tump triggers equally powerful memories for her aunt and her mother, Nellie recalling her heightened awareness of Hugh's thigh occasionally brushing against hers as they dug, and Laura recalling her intense jealousy as she observed her husband and sister working together.

But it is not just emotionally charged places that have this effect. Lively, who as we saw in *The Road to Lichfield* is adept at portraying the associative way the mind works, shows that any random remark or observation can revive dormant memories. For example, what plunges Kate into the memory about the necklace, described earlier, is her coming across a reference to faience beads in an article she is skimming while doing research for one of her exhibits, and what triggers Laura's related memory is her noticing the new junk-shop necklace Kate is wearing when they meet for lunch one day.

Whenever a character descends into memory, the point of view modulates from third person to first person, thereby taking on a more intimate, private quality. Furthermore, the verb tense shifts from past to present, effecting an impression of the immediacy and vividness of the experience being recalled. Often Lively presents a conversation taking place in time present but punctuates it with frequent mental plunges into the past on the part of the characters involved. For instance, in a scene in which Laura and Nellie are looking through an old family picture album with Tom, interwoven with their conversation are glimpses into the sisters' potent memories, occasioned by their coming across a photograph Nellie took of Hugh and Laura the day they announced their engagement to her. The following excerpt begins with Nellie's flashback and concludes with Laura's, with a snatch of conversation sandwiched in between:

They come toward me, walking side by side. There is a wind and it blows Hugh's hair upward from his face, an inverted fringe. I start to say, "Sorry to be so late, there was a . . . [Lively's ellipsis]," and she slips her arm through his, through his crooked elbow, and calls out "You're just in time, Mary's coming over for lunch, and the Sadlers, it's a celebration, Nellie, we've got something to tell you, we're going to get married, Nellie."

He says nothing. They have stopped. He looks wooden, standing beside her. He is wearing gray flannel trousers and a blazer. The trousers are baggy at the knee. I say nothing.

Laura said, "Hugh and me. When can that be? Oh, I remember— you took it, Nellie. That old box Brownie you had. Not long after the war."

Nellie gets out of the car; she is all blown about, she must have driven with the top down, she looks a mess. Hugh's arm is around me; we walk together toward her; I say to him, "Darling, you tell her." I kiss her and say, "You're just in time, it's a celebration, Nellie, Hugh's got something to tell you." Hugh says, "Well, Nellie, there's going to be wedding, we want you to know first of all."

I am wearing my New Look dress—long, long. I feel it brush my calves when I move. It has a petticoat that rustles.

Nellie says, "I'm not entirely surprised. Congratulations. That's marvellous." She takes her suitcase out of the car. She says, "You'll have to learn how to get your hands dirty now, Laura." She goes into the house; there are creases all across the back of her skirt. (*TT*, 26–27)

Scenes such as these, which present snippets of dialogue interrupted by longer, more sustained flashbacks, are abundantly deployed throughout the novel. They create an impression of characters being submerged, fishlike, in the depths of their private pasts, surfacing only occasionally to participate in the present. Lively uses this flashback technique, then, to dramatize the major role memory plays in human consciousness.

Lively's Early Achievement

The title phrase "treasures of time" neatly ties together a number of the novel's major concerns and motifs—the archaeological theme, the focus on various kinds of exploitations of the past, and the demonstration of the wealth of memories characters house in their minds. Like *The Road to Lichfield, Treasures of Time* is an artistically coherent work. With these first two novels, then, Lively established herself as a writer very much in control of her materials. She also launched her reputation for producing books that are at once entertaining social satires and explorations of serious themes. The concerns she addresses in *The Road to Lichfield* and *Treasures of time*—the complexity of our attitudes toward history and toward our own personal pasts, the way memory slumbers in our consciousness, the partial nature of evidence, the subjectivity of our interpretations—will continue to figure in her subsequent fiction, as will the unconventional narrative techniques she introduces in these books.

Chapter Three

Judgment Day

Like *The Road to Lichfield* and *Treasures of Time*, *Judgment Day* (1980) is a highly patterned, artistically coherent work built around a central symbol. Just as "the road to Lichfield" alludes to the journey into the past that concerns the first novel, and "treasures of time" to the various ways characters in the second novel invest in the past, so does the title phrase of the third novel refer to that book's unifying symbol: a fourteenth-century Doom painting entitled "The Day of Judgment," which is on the wall of a medieval church in the village where the novel is set. With its apocalyptic depiction of the division of humankind into the saved and the damned, this painting is an apt emblem for the novel's pervasive themes of fate, luck, and salvation. As with her first two novels, though, Lively never sacrifices the textured "felt life" quality for symbolism or structure; the work's verisimilitude and in-depth characterizations prevent its patterning from becoming obtrusive.

Plot and Characters

Because the point of view in this novel is spread almost equally among a number of main characters, there is no real protagonist per se. As in most of Lively's other novels, however, one character does serve as the major spokesperson for the author's ideas, and that is 35-year-old Clare Paling. Clare bears a strong resemblance to Anne Linton in that she is intellectual and capable but more interested in family and community than in a career. Both women share Lively's interest in history and ecclesiastical architecture, and Clare additionally shares the author's outspoken agnosticism.

Like Anne with her involvement in the Splatt's Cottage Preservation Committee, Clare finds herself caught up in a local preservation campaign. The Palings—Clare, her successful electronics engineer husband, Peter, and their two young children—have recently moved to the Midlands village of Laddenham because of Peter's career advancement (Laddenham is a satellite of the industrial town of Spelbury, where Peter's firm is located). They've bought an Edwardian house facing the village green in the old center of Laddenham; on the other side of the green is the village's historic landmark, the eleventh-century Church of St. Peter and St. Paul. With her children in school all day and her husband frequently away on business trips, Clare finds herself with time on her hands; so when she learns of a local movement to raise funds to renovate the church, she joins. Although not a churchgoer, she appreciates the building for its historical interest and, in particular, for its medieval Doom painting.

The plot revolves around this fund-raising project and the villagers involved with it. Much of the novel's interest derives from these characters, whose points of view are revealed via Lively's usual shifting third-person and kaleidoscopic techniques. As she did in *Treasures of Time,* the author here again demonstrates her skill at creating sympathetic portraits of a wide variety of people.

George Radwell, the vicar, is a brilliant creation. Self-conscious and inept, he is consumed with a Prufrockian awareness of his own failure to amount to anything. Now middle-aged, he looks back on his life and sees a chain of actions characterized by mediocrity and ineffectuality, including his lusterless performance as a student, his choice-by-default to enter the church, his failure to marry, and his social gracelessness. These feelings are intensified when he gets to know Clare Paling. Sure of herself, articulate, and disarming, she is the very antithesis of the vicar, who finds himself becoming doubly clumsy in her presence. The first time he sees her, gazing at the Doom painting in the church,

> he marched down the nave and launched into conversation. Disastrous, as it was to turn out, conversation.
>
> Ah, he said, you must be Mrs Paling, my churchwarden mentioned, Sydney Porter, lives in the corner house, possibly you've come across, also I've noticed the car, nice to have children around, not that I've been twitching the lace curtains, don't think. He laughed; the silly, snorty laugh that always came when he was least sure of himself. Settled in all right, I hope, he continued, very friendly place Laddenham, quite a bit going on one way and another, madrigal society meet at, er, flourishing adult whatsit I'm told, cricket if your husband plays, thought he looked as if possibly, anyway sure you'll find plenty, lot of redecorating I expect, these big Edwardian houses, vicarage badly in need of, know the area already perhaps?
>
> And she ignored all this, not even looking at him most of the time, engrossed still by the Doom.[1]

This speech, presented from George's limited third-person point of view, is obviously not a literal transcription but rather an impressionistic approximation. Lively captures the nervous, inarticulate, rushed quality of the speech but exaggerates these traits to show us how George's words sound to his own self-conscious ears.

As foolish as he is, though, George is not meant to function as merely a figure of fun in the novel. On the contrary, Lively's portrayals of his moments of introspection evoke great compassion. Particularly moving is his gnawing sense of his own isolation. Presiding almost weekly over weddings, funerals, and christenings, he is painfully aware of his own tangential relationship to the big emotional experiences of life. This awareness becomes especially acute when he finds himself sexually attracted to Clare, who pays him barely any attention. His fantasies about making love to her, although humorous in a way, underscore the discrepancy between the life he would like to have and the reality of his empty existence.

Another complex, compassionately drawn character is Sydney Porter, the elderly church warden, who has lived in Laddenham since his retirement from the navy. He is outwardly a quiet, close-mouthed person, a loner who seems to prefer working in his garden to socializing. But as she does with George Radwell, Lively reveals that there is much more to this man than he shows the world. Like George, he has his own private struggles: he constantly tries to suppress the painful memory of losing his wife and small daughter 40 years earlier in the London blitz. From time to time some association causes Sydney to relive that experience, and he becomes filled with terror and an awareness of the randomness of fate. His orderliness—his clockwork daily schedule, his carefully planned garden, his neatly organized house—is a way of keeping the terror at bay, of feeling he has some control over his life.

A third poignantly drawn character is 10-year-old Martin Bryan, who lives next door to Sydney Porter.[2] He too does daily battle with private pain: his is the anxious, insecure existence of an only child in a loveless, joyless home, one frequently rocked by the vicious marital battles of his parents. The latter are so consumed by their own problems and unhappiness that they pay little attention to the affection-starved child. Lively conveys the pathos of the boy's situation not by direct authorial comment but, more effectively and understatedly, through the child's own thoughts, which reveal his desperate need for parental attention. For example, when his father runs off for a few days with his girlfriend, forgetting all about his promise to take Martin to the Air Show, the child displaces his affection to the bike his father gave him: "He'd got the new bike anyway. The red bike. The bike Dad sent" (*JD,* 132). And when he doesn't hear from his father, he tries to reassure himself: "There hadn't been any postcards from Dad; perhaps he was in a place where they didn't have interesting postcards. That was probably why" (*JD,* 154). Lively deftly portrays the desperate struggles of a young child grappling with emotions he cannot articulate or analyze.

Clare, a more familiar type in Lively's fiction than are George, Sydney, and Martin, differs from them in that she is not afflicted with personal problems. On the contrary, she is extraordinarily lucky: good-looking, intelligent, well-to-do, happily married, and blessed with healthy, well-adjusted children whom she adores. Although there is a sharpness in Clare's manner that makes her less appealing than some of Lively's other female spokespersons (such as Anne Linton), this impression is softened by the revelations of her private thoughts, which show her to be disturbed by her own off-putting manner and uncomfortably aware of her greater than average share of blessings. In fact, it is primarily through Clare's reflections about the random, unfair distribution of fortunes and misfortunes that Lively expresses the book's themes about fate and luck, which will be discussed in this chapter.

There are times when Clare borders on being a mouthpiece for Lively's ideas about history, fate, and agnosticism (although it is probably only readers like myself, who are well acquainted with all Lively's fiction and opinions, who tend to see Clare this way), but the fullness of her characterization prevents this from happening. Particularly convincing is the portrayal of Clare's maternal emotions. Like many another of Lively's female protagonists, Clare is prone to moments of intense, overwhelming tenderness for her offspring and astonishment at the miracle of their existence. Her glance alighting on the head of her small son, Thomas, for example, she suddenly experiences a "melting of the vitals produced by the sight of the back of his neck, of such downy delicacy that one never ceases to marvel" (*JD,* 72). It is details like these that render Clare very human and prevent her from becoming the mere vehicle for ideas she sometimes threatens to become.

These four characters—George, Sydney, Martin, and Clare—are given the greatest coverage in the novel, but there are a number of others whose points of view are also presented. As the action proceeds the characters become increasingly involved with one another, at first because of the community effort to raise funds for the church and then because of a string of accidents and tragedies that draw people together. The last two of these rock the community profoundly, occurring as they do in the immediate neighborhood and in rapid succession: first, on the night before the planned fund-raising performance, the church is vandalized by a gang of hoodlums, forcing the cancellation of the event; then the very next day young Martin Bryan is fatally struck by a motorcycle while bike riding with the Paling children in front of the church. Both disasters are blatant reminders of the randomness and cruelty of fate, themes with which the novel has been concerned and which are symbolized by the central image of the Doom painting. It is thus fitting that the novel ends with the vicar reading the church restoration expert's report and noting its recommendation that the painting "The Day of Judgment," above all else, be restored and preserved.

History

Lively's historical sensibility pervades this novel, as it does all of her others. With her usual eye for the palimpsest, layered quality of place, she draws attention to the pastiche of periods embodied in the architecture of Laddenham: the village is a "muddled place," "its strata confused" (*JD*, 1), with modern estates scattered among 1930s semis (semidetached houses) and Victorian terraced cottages. Although the homogenizing effects of modern urban development have made Laddenham indistinguishable in many ways from numerous other English towns, each with its Boots, Dewhurst, Tesco, and so on, the spirit of place can still be detected: in the name of the village, which "hitches it still to a past" (*JD*, 1); in the odd local expression or accent that surfaces from time to time out of the otherwise unplaceable, classless English most of the inhabitants now speak; and in certain older buildings that are a "reminder that this place lay on the limestone spine of England, and was built from its own bones" (*JD*, 26). Most notable among these last is the eleventh-century Church of St. Peter and St. Paul. With an Amoco station situated on one side of it and a car park on the other, this edifice is a striking example of the juxtaposition of periods that characterizes modern British towns. It is also a symbolic reminder of the presence of the past.

The villagers have long taken the church for granted, its parishioners regarding it as simply a place of worship and not as a historic monument. But then controversial Clare Paling enters the community and stirs up the vicar and other church members with her argument that the way to raise money for restoration is to draw the public's attention to the building's historical, rather than spiritual, significance. This suggestion sets off a recurring debate between Clare and other committee members concerning the way the church's historical past should be depicted. And Lively uses the debate to voice, via Clare, her by now familiar views about history and our attitudes toward it.

The popular tendency to prettify history, which Lively of course is critical of, is demonstrated by a committee member named Miss Bellingham, who keeps insisting that the pageant ought to feature maypole dancing and quaint medieval costumes. Clare counters the woman's suggestions with Lively-like sentiments, such as "That's not history. . . . History is ghastly. Nothing but misery and war and brutality" (*JD*, 48), and "In the Middle Ages, . . . they boiled people in oil. They also dropped them off castles, impaled them and flayed them alive. It wasn't universally charming" (*JD*, 133). Aware, like Anne Linton and Tom Rider, that this idealizing of history keeps it from seeming real to people, Clare convinces the others that the pageant ought to dramatize some of the unattractive realities of the church's past, specifically the Cromwellian execution of dissenters that took place in the churchyard during the Civil War and a nineteenth-century riot by local farmers demanding higher wages that involved destroying part of the church's edifice and resulted in their being sentenced and transported.

Clare also takes issue with the tendency to regard history as something that happened long ago, pointing out that if far enough removed in time, the horrors of the past take on a certain fascination for people: "the sufferings of others—especially if comfortably in the past—[have] proven drawing power" (*JD*, 84). She offers as evidence the huge crowds that flock to the Tower of London every year, echoing her author, who has cited the popularity of the Tower and of the London Dungeon as examples of the deplorable fad of treating history as entertainment (Interview). This notion that history is safely shut away in books and museums is exposed as an illusion in the course of the novel. Although toward the beginning Clare observes that "most of us aren't even conscious that [history is] going on" (*JD*, 20), by the end of the novel the onslaught of disasters has made the villagers aware that they are indeed a part of history.

Sydney Porter arrives at this insight in the same kind of sudden epiphany Lively herself experienced when she grasped the reality of the past. Doing research for the fund-raising pageant, he spends an afternoon reading about the local church's scarred, violent past, and "when he finished he was oddly shaken; involved, as though what he'd been reading was fiction, novels, thrillers—not things in history books, over and done with. You never thought of all that as having to do with you personally. You never thought of yourself as being part of the same process. Now, . . . thinking of Podd and Lacy and Binns [the striking farmers who were transported], he saw suddenly an unending remorseless sequence; people harried and cut down, Christians, Jews, fanatics, prophets, stubborn religious soldiers, disgruntled country labourers, Mary and Jennifer [his wife and daughter]" (*JD*, 68–69). Another character, Sue Coggan, comes close to having a similar insight when a fatal air disaster occurs just a few miles away. Less reflective than Clare and Sydney, she gropes to express her reaction: "I could hardly believe it, when it came on the news. I mean, you don't expect things like that on your own doorstep, do you? It made me feel quite funny for a minute" (*JD*, 113).

With one disaster piled upon another, Lively drives home the point that the horrors of history are not over. Contemporary disasters are simply modern-day manifestations of the same primitive evil that has menaced humankind down through the ages. A dream Sydney has illustrates this point dramatically: it mingles the visual images of an earlier evil— the World War II bombing that killed his wife and daughter—with the sounds of a currently occurring one—motorcycle hoodlums vandalizing the green and smashing Sydney's front door light while he sleeps. Sydney's unconscious forges all these sensations into a coherent scenario in which the motorcycles' zoom becomes the sound of the bombs exploding and the lightbulb crashing becomes that of the windows breaking in his old home in London. The connection between past evil and present evil becomes even more apparent when the hoodlums strike a second time, the night before the planned pageant, wreaking destruction on the church in an eerie real-life reenactment of the violence that was to have been dramatically reenacted the following evening. Clare perceives this connection when she first lays eyes on the wreckage the next morning: "How very Cromwellian," she observes (*JD*, 151). The villagers now find themselves involved with actual history rather than imitation history. History, then, is suddenly real for them.

Judgment Day

Judgment Day begins and ends with the focus on the fourteenth-century Doom painting on the wall of the village church, and there are numerous references and allusions to this painting throughout the novel. The image of all souls being divided up into the blessed and the damned haunts many of the characters, Clare in particular, and forms a symbolic backdrop to the novel's action. Although the painting was intended to remind illiterate medieval congregations of the "brevity and insecurity of life and the perils of non-repentance" (*JD,* 65), it has an equally powerful impact on modern-day viewers holding a vastly different worldview and lacking the burning faith of the Middle Ages. The modern agnostic world is just as aware of the precariousness of life and the unequal distribution of fortune, and just as guilt-ridden; the difference is that we cannot take comfort, as could our forebears, in the belief in a divine plan and ultimate justice.

In a manner reminiscent of Thomas Hardy, Lively emphasizes the randomness of fortune.[3] Clare frequently articulates her view that the world seems to be arbitrarily divided up into the lucky and the unlucky, and she is guiltily conscious of belonging to the former group. The novel's characters are deployed so as to illustrate this division: lucky Clare, with her intellectual, physical, and financial resources and her possession of a fulfilling family life, is surrounded by people painfully lacking all or some of these blessings—most obviously, George, Sydney, and Martin. Clare is also hyperconscious of the way disasters seem to strike from out of the blue; she is prone to picturing worst-case scenarios and she gravitates toward newspaper stories about quirky accidents and undeserved tragedies. Her outlook is vindicated when the hitherto tranquil village of Laddenham suddenly finds itself visited by a series of such events, including fatal and near-fatal accidents and the increasingly menacing acts of the motorcycle gang. As a result, by the end of the novel not only Clare but the other villagers as well have a heightened sense of the precariousness of life and of human powerlessness against the vagaries of fate.

The visitations of evil on the community echo the apocalyptic images in the Doom painting. In an elaborate motif, Lively links the red devils depicted in the painting leading souls into hell with the motorcycle gang, as well as with a team of R.A.F. display planes based in nearby Willerton that occasionally rupture the bucolic peacefulness with their deafening, terrifying noise as they zoom across the sky. These planes are actually called the Red Devils, and George makes the initial connection between them and the pictorial red devils in a joking way, when he attempts to say something clever to Clare the first time he comes upon her gazing at the painting. But the connection becomes more significant when Clare, on a rural outing near Willerton, witnesses the display team practicing. In an almost apocalyptic scene, one "huge scarlet steel dart" after another shoots across the sky, awing and overwhelming Clare with "the sudden intrusion, the sense of something quite merciless and irresistible blasting its way across the tranquil countryside." It stirs her up strangely, causing her to drive home "too fast, narrowly missing an accident, the sight of the red aeroplanes still printed on her eyeballs" (*JD*, 28)—an intricate foreshadowing of the accident she does eventually have later in the summer when, similarly exhilarated, she is driving too fast on her way to the air show, an accident that ironically prevents her from attending this event at which one of the Red Devils crashes and kills several people.

Clare subsequently makes a connection between the Red Devils and the menacing motorcycle gang when she catches a glimpse of the latter a few days after witnessing the display team's practice: "the motorbike boys roared past, an explosion of noise and wake of acrid smell, reminding her of those aeroplanes" (*JD*, 50). And like the planes, they ultimately perpetrate violence and destruction upon the community. Clare looks at their acts of vandalism in symbolic, universal terms, regarding them as "the unleashing of some elemental force, sinister and uncontrollable" (*JD*, 127). This reaction is similar to George Radwell's—"what they had done was as elemental and impersonal as weather—a hurricane, a flood" (*JD*, 156)—and echoes Clare's earlier description of the Red Devils as "something quite merciless and irresistible" (*JD*, 28). The various, disparate manifestations of evil in the novel are thus all linked to the same sinister force depicted in the Doom painting.

Like Clare, most of the other main characters come to see this link. On several occasions Sydney Porter reflects on the underlying connection of all of history's evils. For example, while he is reading about the violent local events of the seventeenth and nineteenth centuries as part of his research for the historical pageant,

> images came and went in his mind like a series of projector slides: Podd and Lacy and Binns, ragged ineffectual figures with country accents herded into some creaking ship; troops streaming up the gangway of the *Ranchi* at Portsmouth in 1940, hung about with kit, waving three deep from the rails; the dust and debris and broken glass in [his former home in] Mansell Road, Mary's plaster-whitened hair. He saw people hustled hither and thither, blown by terrible mindless winds, helpless, hapless. He saw too, suddenly, the wall-painting in the church and the grey figures bundled away by red devils or stern condescending angels. (*JD*, 65)

Later, while watching a rehearsal of the pageant, he finds himself gazing at the wall painting and sees "its details more sharply than perhaps ever before: the grey spectral figures, the spry grinning red devils. He didn't believe in hell himself, nor heaven either, not put like that. But, looking at the painting, he heard again the whine of bombs in Portsmouth harbour, the rattle of gunfire at sea, saw the smoking shell of Mansell Road" (*JD,* 135). Similarly, George Radwell is flooded with a series of mental images linking current evils to the Doom painting: in shock after the accident that kills Martin Bryan, he stands "staring at the dresser, seeing many things. . . . Wheels and Anna Paling's crumpled face [as she witnessed Martin's accident] and, for some reason, a part of the wall-painting in the church" (*JD,* 159).

Existential Anxiety

As cruel and primitive as it is, the vision of life expressed in the Doom painting is thus not far removed from that held by most of the novel's main characters. Again, though, the difference is that they cannot believe, as could the painting's original audience, that there is a divine reason behind the apparently arbitrary blows of fortune and the predestination of souls. The novel is an exploration of the way contemporary people, lacking such faith, cope with the apparent metaphysical meaninglessness and structurelessness of existence.

Lively presents us with an array of approaches. There is, for example, smug Sue Coggan who operates by denying the essentially uncontrollable nature of life. Methodically filling in her calendar months in advance ("Car for 6,000 mile service," "Holiday bookings," "Dad's birthday"), she creates the illusion of having control over her future, right down to planning the exact date of bringing another child into the world: "if we have another next year, when Tracy's just turned six, October would be best, well after the summer holidays and before Christmas, so I'd be up and about in good time for the shopping. Three's a nice number—two girls and a little boy" (*JD,* 14). To this last plan she quickly appends "touch wood, cross fingers"—a concession, albeit somewhat perfunctory, to the fact that there are a few things, the sex of an unborn child being one, over which she has no control. It is ironic that as she is ruminating on these plans she happens to notice Martin Bryan playing outside, for the tragedy that will befall him in a few weeks is a dramatic reminder of how little control one really does have over the life of a child. And closer to home, Sue's child will suffer a potentially fatal accident—getting an object lodged in her nose—that jolts Sue out of her complacency.

Whereas Sue Coggan usually manages to avert her eyes from the chaotic nature of reality, Martin Bryan is acutely aware of it, no doubt in good part because of the chaos of his own immediate reality—his family life. He has the tendency, shared by certain of Lively's later characters, to slip into a state of psychological disorientation in which he feels untethered from the basic cognitive moorings of time and space. For example, walking home from school one day, he suddenly "couldn't remember what day it was. He stopped dead, outside the butcher's . . . and didn't know if it was Tuesday or Thursday or what. His head whirled. You needed to know things like that, it was like knowing who you were yourself: Martin Keith Bryan, aged ten, 3 The Green, Laddenham, nr. Spelbury, Oxfordshire, England, Europe, The World, the Universe" (*JD,* 30–31). He is paralyzed by anxiety until he works out what day it is: "Once more placed in time, he was able to start walking again" (*JD,* 31). Martin, then, desperately clings to the structures of time and space to restrain his tendency toward existential vertigo.

Some of the characters express this same basic anxiety in the form of a hyperawareness of the possibility of random disaster. The vicar's agoraphobic housekeeper, Mrs. Tanner, for instance, is so obsessed with this possibility that she is afraid to ride on trains and buses, to go near the sea, and even to walk down the street alone. Although this eccentric character is no doubt included partly for comic effect, she does serve the thematic purpose of drawing attention to the randomness of fate. George's counsel to her, although intended to help her gain perspective, unintentionally corroborates her outlook: "all those things are the same for everyone. For all of us. I mean, the chances. It's—well, just the risk of being alive at all" (*JD,* 43).

Whereas Mrs. Tanner's preoccupation with disaster grows out of a phobia, Sydney Porter's is a product of his actual life experiences. Not as extreme as Mrs. Tanner's, his way of coping is to withdraw into a minimalist existence—"He had lost everything. For the rest of his life he would have nothing, so that that might never happen again. No more love; no more commitment. They can't take away from you what you haven't got. He would live on the foothills, expect little and risk little" (*JD,* 66)—and to exert excessive control over those things that can be controlled: his gardening, his housekeeping, and his daily schedule. He also turns to the Church, but not for the traditional reason of finding solace and answers in religion. Like all of the novel's characters, he is incapable of the faith of bygone days; instead, it is the orderliness of the Church that attracts him. This is revealed in his recollection of the priest who tried to console him after the death of his wife and child:

> The padre would bumble on and grind eventually to a halt, and Sydney would nod and then there'd be a silence; both of them, Sydney supposed, not being fools, knew that in the end there was nothing to be said. The padre talked of faith and the comfort of prayer and the love of God; he talked to Sydney as one believer to another. What he didn't know, could never have explained, was that it was order Sydney sought, and found, in the Church, rather than any of that. The order of things said and done each time in the same way, the order of knowing that nothing could interfere with how those things were said and done, the knowledge that this order had gone before and would go on after, that it survived the chaos of everything else. (*JD,* 66)

Even the vicar lacks the certainty of traditional religious faith. His involvement with the Church sprang originally from a typing mistake: in writing up the college intentions of the sixth form students, the secretary at his old school had typed in "Theological" for "Technical" next to the name George Radwell. One thing led to another and George, ever ineffectual and unassertive, found himself propelled into a career in the Church, eventually taking comfort not in faith but in the sense of being part of something larger than himself. The Church becomes a refuge for him to hide in. Counseling parishioners and administering weddings, funerals, and christenings, he gives the appearance of being involved with life and other people, but he runs none of the emotional risks of real involvement. In a sense, then, he is coping the same way Sydney is—by opting to "live on the foothills" (*JD,* 66).

Finally, Clare Paling, although outwardly strong and fearless, is another character who experiences a gnawing awareness of the riskiness of life, as is evidenced by her obsession with disasters. A thoroughgoing agnostic, she is annoyed when people attribute either tragic or fortuitous events to the will of God. In response to a remark that the car accident that prevented her and the children from attending the air show where the fatal crash occurred was a deliverance and not a haphazard coincidence, she retorts, "If the hand of God twitched my car out of the way of that lorry yesterday, then it also threw an aeroplane on top of six other people including a three year old child and a pregnant woman. If there is someone around who does things like that, then I want no part of whoever or whatever he, she or it may be" (*JD,* 119).

Clare is the only character who bluntly acknowledges the absence of ultimate causes and patterns in the universe. And yet despite her out-spoken existentialism, she too feels the need for something to rely on. She finds this in language; language is in a sense Clare's religion. Significantly, when she decides to attend a church service and to read the Bible to her children, it is because of her attraction to the words—to the rhythms and connotations of the Biblical phrases—rather than to the content. For this reason she is dismayed to discover that since she last attended a service, several years earlier, the traditional Book of Common Prayer and Authorized Version of the Bible have been replaced by alternative texts written in a more accessible, straightforward modern style, a style Clare feels lacks the power and majesty of the original. When she complains about this to the vicar, he counters, "I shouldn't have thought it would matter to you all that much, . . . as a non-believer. . . . It's only words, after all." Clare's response is highly reveal-ing: "Only words? *Only* words! Oh, dear. But you see, words are what I do believe in. They're all we've got" (*JD,* 83).

Clare, then, like most of the other characters, displays a basic existen-tial anxiety that is a product of the modern agnostic outlook to which Lively subscribes. Like their medieval forebears, these characters are sen-sitive to the inequities and random evils that befall human existence, but unlike the former, they cannot believe there is an ultimate metaphysical pattern to or purpose behind this chaos. And thus they struggle to develop various coping strategies, such as clinging to the human con-structs of time, space, and language or creating the illusion of order and safety in their own domestic spheres.

Lively's Secular Humanism

Judgment Day's portrayal of a spectrum of contemporary responses to the vagaries of fate and the uncertainties of existence has caused one review-er to label it a "modern-day morality play."[4] There is indeed a kind of archetypal, "Everyman" quality to the novel, with its cluster of charac-ters representing different ages and stations in life grouped around an ancient village green and the church looming over and uniting them. But this is a modern morality play, and Lively is exploring the question of how we can live moral, meaningful lives in a world without religious imperatives.

It is mainly through Clare that the author addresses this issue. The two hold the same philosophical and moral outlook, which Clare sums up for George Radwell in the following way: "I believe, . . . insofar as I believe anything, that we are quite fortuitously here, and that the world is a cruel and terrible place, but inexplicably and bewilderingly beautiful" (*JD,* 119). It is this beauty that is the world's salvation, and moments in which one apprehends it are presented as spiritually redemptive. For Clare these moments usually take the form of an almost mystical insight into the "marvelous presence of the physical world" (*JD,* 106) or an unexpected soulful connection with another human being.

Ironically, although Clare is the most outspoken of all the characters about her lack of religious belief, she is in a sense the most spiritual. She is the most prone to the kind of epiphany described above, and it is she who has the only clear vision of the way to redemption in the modern agnostic world: "I believe that people are capable of great good and great evil, and ought to be good. And I believe that the capacity for love is the greatest we have. Every kind of love. Kindness or charity or tolerance or whatever you care to call it." When George, to whom she has made this declaration, responds, "You sound like a Christian," she corrects him, "Oh no. Because I believe that when we die we die and that is that" (*JD,* 119). It is, in other words, a secular humanist vision that Clare—like Lively—holds. In the course of the novel the other characters come around to this view, as they find themselves opening up emotionally to one another. It is therefore significant that the first time the vicar sees Clare, standing in a shaft of sunlight gazing at the wall painting, he endows her with a spiritual significance, perceiving her as "bathed in gold like a stained glass Virgin" (*JD,* 2).

When Clare moves to Laddenham, she enters a community in which people dwell side by side without really knowing one another, each house "an island unto itself" (*JD,* 101). Most of the main characters live very private lives, harboring secret pains and problems that their neighbors are unaware of. But Clare's entrance into the village changes all this. Her proposal that the church raise funds by putting on a historical pageant sets off a chain of events that will spawn a number of meaningful friendships over the course of the novel.

The first emotional connection that occurs is between Clare and Sydney Porter. Thrown together because they are the only two interested in doing the historical research for the fund-raising pageant, the incongruous pair are initially uncomfortable with one each other. But then one afternoon while they are making strained conversation over a cup of tea, Sydney suddenly perceives that Clare is embarrassed and realizes that there is a vulnerable human being behind her brisk, confident facade and that she is "quite a nice woman, really, even if a bit off-putting with that sharp way of talking and a strung-up feeling about her, as though she had to hold herself back all the time" (*JD*, 67). This insight triggers a breakthrough in their relationship, as Sydney proceeds to open up to her about his wife and daughter—something he rarely does—because he senses that she will understand. She does, and the conversation marks the beginning of a sustained friendship between the two.

The experience of relating to Clare seems to make Sydney more open to forming other emotional connections, for soon after this he experiences a similar breakthrough in his attitude toward George Radwell. The two men have met almost daily in the course of their church-related work for over a dozen years, but never has their relationship swerved from its formal, professional track. They are vicar and warden, not friends. Then one day Sydney suddenly, and for the first time, really *sees* the vicar and is flooded with understanding of him:

> [George] said again, twice, that he must be getting on, and did not. . . . It came to Sydney, all of a sudden, that the vicar was a lonely man as well as one who could never be done with what he was saying or say what he meant to any effect. He seemed, standing there with his sandy hair and his pink face, like one of those diffident small boys who lurk on the edges of a playground, not invited to join in, while all around people are whooping and shrieking. Poor bastard, Sydney thought. It was one thing to have chosen that sort of life: another to have been shoved into it by circumstance. Because you were a bit of a ham-handed bloke with a silly laugh. It was one thing to have turned your back on involvement, quite another never to have known it. (*JD*, 97)

But by far the most important emotional connection Sydney makes is with young Martin Bryan. In all the 10 years the two have lived next door to each other, Sydney has barely exchanged a word with the strange, quiet child. Therefore when Martin's irresponsible mother, Shirley, asks Sydney if he wouldn't mind keeping an eye on the lad for a few days while both parents are away, it is with great trepidation that he agrees. But over the course of their week together, they gradually fall into a companionable routine, with Sydney teaching Martin to hoe and plant and the two sharing a nightly cup of cocoa in front of the television or over a game of cards. Their friendship, which continues even after Mrs. Bryan returns home, becomes primary to both: Sydney fulfills the little boy's craving for fatherly attention and Martin gives the old man

someone and something to live for—other than his garden—for the first
time in almost 40 years.

The most significant of all the emotional connections formed in
Judgment Day is that between the vicar and Clare. Throughout most of
the novel the gap between the two is enormous: he places her high on a
pedestal, convinced of the unattainability of a woman like her for a man
like him, and she regards him dismissively and contemptuously. But
then she experiences the same kind of breakthrough in understanding of
him that Sydney did earlier: when she finally notices that he is attracted
to her, she reacts not with disgust or scorn but with pity, for she suddenly grasps what life must be like for someone like George Radwell, "being
inadequate and knowing you are inadequate and failing to attract anything more vital than indifference from other people and probably
knowing that too. And having presumably the normal instincts towards
love and lust and other kinds of emotional participation but, apparently,
neither wife nor children nor family nor friends. Nobody ever goes into
the vicarage except on church business" (*JD*, 126). From that moment
on she is more sensitive to him, and at one point comes to his rescue
when, during a pageant rehearsal, the director and actors are smirking at
him and his suggestions: "there had come a point when she could no
longer loiter in the shelter of the nave, idly watching; when, suddenly,
the spectacle of George Radwell making things worse for himself with
every blundering remark had become intolerable. Persecution will not
do, even of those who invite it" (*JD*, 139).

Clare and George finally achieve real friendship when they recognize
their equality. At the end of the novel, brought together in their efforts
to deal with the aftermath of the village's recent disasters, Clare suddenly realizes that the experience has made her regard George differently:
"It came to her as extraordinary that they had moved together, she and
this man, through the previous day; like being trapped with a stranger
in a lift. But he was not, now, a stranger. . . . I don't dislike George
Radwell any more" (*JD*, 162). She proceeds to invite him home for
lunch, and for the first time the two relate as equals, with George conversing without stuttering and Clare acknowledging the validity of his
points. In a gesture carrying the same symbolic significance as Sydney's
opening up to Clare about Mary and Jennifer, Clare offers, indirectly, to
go to bed with George. And, equally significantly, he declines the offer.

In addition to these spiritually redemptive connections made between
individuals, the village as a whole experiences a kind of spiritual com-

munal bonding. And just as in a traditional morality play, it is the church that brings the villagers together and provides transcendence. This role is symbolized by the awesome, ethereal appearance the building takes on when, the night before the planned pageant, the floodlighting is turned on and the inhabitants of the houses around the green, including agnostic Clare, find their eyes riveted by the spectacle. Even though the villagers' involvement with it is for secular reasons—the producing of the historical pageant—St. Peter and St. Paul has been the instrument of spiritual redemption for the community. George notes this when everyone gathers to clean up the church the day after it is vandalized: although their plans have been ruined and they face an ordeal of hard work ahead, "never before had [the vicar] known the church so filled with goodwill" (*JD,* 152). In the aftermath of the tragedies and disasters that have befallen the community—events that underscore the powerlessness of human beings and the blindness of fate—the villagers seem to find comfort and salvation in the idea that, as Clare has voiced it, "We are in the world with other people" (*JD,* 162).

Conclusion

Treating the same general themes of history, the past, and subjectivity that the first two novels do, *Judgment Day* also gives expression to a less prominent facet of Lively's outlook that emerges from time to time in her fiction: the existential anxiety—often experienced by characters as an uneasy sense of being cut loose from the moorings of quotidian reality—that seems to be an outgrowth of the author's agnosticism. Martin's fear of losing his grip on the familiar cognitive structures of time and space and Clare's desperate clinging to language as the one certainty in an otherwise meaningless universe prefigure the anxieties of forthcoming characters. As we shall see, the metaphors "untethered" and "adrift" occur repeatedly in Lively's fiction.

But as *Judgment Day* demonstrates, although the world of Lively's fiction contains some dark and terrifying elements, it is not finally a bleak place. It is kept from so becoming by the author's secular humanism— her compassion for and delight in human beings, her conviction of their basic decency, and her belief in their ability to connect profoundly with one another. The darkness is also redeemed by those gracelike moments of insight into life's beauty and significance that descend occasionally on Lively's characters.

Chapter Four

Next to Nature, Art

Next to Nature, Art (1982) is a very different kind of novel from Lively's others, particularly its immediate predecessor. It lacks the depth of characterization and the intimate probing of consciousnesses of the others, as well as their overriding concerns with history, memory, and subjectivity. Instead, this novel is more in keeping with a type of Lively's short stories: the crisp, pointed satire that exposes the pretentiousness of a particular class of people. Satiric scenes are sprinkled throughout Lively's other novels, but *Next to Nature, Art* is the only one in which the satiric predominates. The author's target is the narcissistic artists she has frequently criticized: those who, according to Lively, "strike up attitudes, who think that being creative gives them a licence to behave badly" (Chia, 2). Although some reviewers find this novel to be heavy-handed in its moralism and satire,[1] most regard it as a witty, entertaining work that deftly captures the speech and mannerisms of its satirical targets.

Plot, Characters, and Satire

The novel is set in 1974, "a time," points out the sarcastic narrator, "when creativity is rated high,"[2] and it concerns one of those residential art courses that were so popular during that era. Toby Standish, the 40-year-old scion of an ancient Warwickshire family, has converted his going-to-seed ancestral home, Framleigh Hall, into an artists' commune and workshop called the Framleigh Creative Study Centre. Besides Toby, who is a painter, the live-in Framleigh faculty consist of a recent art school graduate named Nick (the only sympathetically portrayed member of the staff), a beautiful sculptor named Paula, a potter named Bob, and an American poet named Greg. Also living at Framleigh is Toby and Paula's out-of-wedlock child, six-year-old Jason.

Into this bohemian setting enter 11 middle-class people who have signed on for one of Framleigh's weeklong creative courses. Lively uses the well-known satirical device of isolating a group of individuals—on an island or a ship or, as in this case, a country house—and observing them disintegrate into their worst selves. Although at first the course members are starry-eyed about being in the midst of "real artists" and about escaping from their philistine lives into the rarified atmosphere of Framleigh, by the end of the week they have become disillusioned, having witnessed the hypocrisy and pretentiousness of most of the Framleigh staff and having watched themselves become increasingly irritable, envious, and competitive. As the narrator points out, the guests come to realize "that they have not been as thoroughly detached from ordinary life as they would have wished" (*NNA*, 111).

Indeed, Lively shows that beneath the counterculture facade of the Framleigh faculty lurk thoroughly bourgeois attitudes. Despite their avowed disdain for middle-class concerns, these bohemians are as mercantile and competitive as the capitalists they despise and as eaten up with sexual jealousy and possessiveness as ordinary, "unliberated" people. Toby, for example, claims that his reason for starting the Framleigh Centre was to establish a creative sanctuary where art and artists could flourish, whereas in reality (we learn from the omniscient narrator), his motive was economic. Further, the communal principles on which he claims to run Framleigh are belied by his actions: his secret financial dealings, his habit of pulling rank, and his exploiting the course members' idealism about communal living to save money on domestic help.

Bob, Greg, and Paula are almost as hypocritical as Toby. Bob secretly runs a profitable sideline in toby jugs and other commercially popular ceramic works, while pretending to produce only carefully crafted William Morris–type pieces. Greg and Paula claim to revere art above all else, but their self-obsessed speech and actions reveal that their real interest is promoting themselves. Greg, for example, indulges in a ludicrously pretentious form of multimedia poetry in which he films himself free-associating about his own creative processes. Paula creates equally ludicrous, narcissistic "sculptures," possessing titles like "Introspective Woman" and fashioned out of such materials as bicycle frames, nylon tights, fruit netting, and so on—sculptures that, as one of the more astute course members wryly observes, "don't somehow add to your vision of anything except possibly old tights or chicken wire or pieces of broken mirror" (*NNA*, 83). Finally, although all of the Framleigh artists pride themselves on their open relationships, this life-style has clearly trapped rather than liberated them: Paula is jealous of Toby's sporadic homosexual relationship with Nick and insecure about her own sexual but uncommitted relationship with Greg; Toby feels oppressed by Nick's dependence on him; Nick suffers agonies as he watches Toby flirt with one of the course members; and nearly all of the faculty get themselves into sticky situations by going to bed with course members and thereby leading them on.

The reader, who bears witness to the faculty members' private conversations and actions, is aware from the beginning that the "Framleigh Ideal" of brotherhood and creativity touted by Toby is a sham. But for the course members, lacking such omniscience, it takes a series of disappointments and disillusionments to arrive at this same realization. These range from their discovery that the Framleigh swimming pool featured in the course brochure is actually a weed-infested eyesore that hasn't been used in decades to their dawning awareness of the staff members' selfishness and shallowness. It is therefore with relief and a new appreciation of their ordinary, responsible lives that most of them conclude their stay at Framleigh.

Narrative and Satiric Techniques

Lively's narrative technique in this novel is somewhat of a departure from the one she ordinarily employs. Although she does her usual roving from character to character, she does not delve as much into characters' intimate thought processes and subjective points of view as she does in her other novels. Instead, she presents characters more objectively and externally, relying largely on omniscient narration and short, revealing dramatic scenes.

An authoritative, cynical voice pervades this novel. Although we get some raw exposures to characters' thoughts, for the most part the narrator tells us things about characters that they themselves could not or would not express. For example, the narrator confides in us, "Once upon a time, Toby and Paula loved one another. Up to a point and in so far as either was prepared to give way to an emotion which does make great demands on egotistic natures. Over the years, love or its equivalent has shrivelled (both have found alternatives for that, in any case) and the relationship now rests on self-interest, a capacity with which Toby and Paula are both healthily endowed. They find each other convenient" (*NNA,* 88). Such an approach is effective for the author's purpose in this novel, which is to satirize and criticize rather than to enlarge our sympathies, as is her aim in most of her other novels. Had Lively presented characters like Toby and Paula from their own point of view, she would have run the risk of making them seem more human and more sympathetic, as happens, for example, in *Treasures of Time* with the otherwise despicable Laura Paxton.

Lively's use of brief dramatic scenes is another device that keeps us from getting close to characters and that maintains a satiric slant. In these scenes, Lively lets the characters' words, thoughts, and actions speak for themselves, and the effect is often highly amusing. For example, in an episode in which Paula has just finished helping Greg film himself doing one of his autobiographical free-association poems, the author manages through dialogue alone to expose a number of negative facts about the two characters: their self-centeredness, their ignorance about what poetry really is, Greg's mediocrity and inarticulateness as a poet, and his foolish, pretentious way of speaking. The excerpt begins with Paula's comment:

> "Of course. The bit about your early work was marvellous. Actually it was just how I felt when I first got into sculpture, that wonderful feeling that now at last one was . . ."
> "Right," says Greg. "What about the final section?"
> "It was great. It's the directness that's so marvellous. And the way you sort of don't quite say things."! [exclamation mark mine]
> "It's what I'm all about," says Greg simply. (*NNA,* 28)

Not all the scenes are this exterior; those featuring decent, sensible characters, like plain-spoken course member Mary Chambers, tend to do more probing of characters' thoughts. But the novel as a whole nonetheless has a kind of surface, cinematic quality, as if a roving camera were recording the goings-on of the various faculty and course members throughout the week. This effect is enhanced by the brief, clipped quality of the scenes—some are only a sentence or a paragraph long—and by their being cast in the present tense. Readers who are drawn to Lively for her in-depth character studies and for her exploration of subjective states of consciousness may find this technique frustrating and unsatisfying. But it is successful in creating the distancing effect needed for satire and hence appropriate for Lively's purpose in this novel.

The Novel's Moralism

Although cynical and at times biting, the satire of *Next to Nature, Art* basically falls into the constructive, Horatian mode, with the author's primary purpose being moral instruction. Indeed, in this novel Lively expresses her values more explicitly than she does in any other. And these values are the traditional humanist ones of personal honesty and decency, responsibility to others, appreciation of nature, and respect for art and ideas.

Lively's main way of conveying these values is through the negative examples of most of the Framleigh staff. Numerous conversations and dramatic scenarios reveal the true colors of these selfish, pretentious people. For example, we see that Toby's reaction is irritation rather than concern when an elderly guest slips on a rock and receives a concussion during a tour of the grounds ("Christ," Toby grumbles. "That's all one needed. These courses are enough of a strain without anything idiotic like this" [*NNA,* 46]); we witness Bob tucking away his own private bottle purchased with the money he secretly earns from his toby jugs; we listen to Greg lie about receiving a fellowship in creative writing from an American university; and we note how on a tour of an ancient cathedral, while Keith (one of the course members) displays genuine interest in the medieval architecture, Paula is interested in the subject only insofar as it relates to herself (in response to Keith's knowledgeable remarks, she "stares at him, and says the texture of the stone is gorgeous, and as a matter of fact she used it as the model for some rather intriguing ceramic work last year" [*NNA,* 92]).

Pitted against the negative examples of Toby, Paula, Greg, and Bob is the positive example of one of the course members, a middle-aged woman named Mary Chambers. She possesses many of the qualities that Lively's readers have come to expect in her likable female characters: she is sensible, no-nonsense, knowledgeable about nature, and unaffectedly interested in art and ideas. From the beginning we recognize her as the novel's moral authority. She is the first of the course members to see through the Framleigh staff, noting almost immediately the way they try to set themselves up as superior by "appearing not to care or even be interested in what other people think of [them] and wearing clothes that are superficially like the clothes everyone else is wearing but also subtly not, and talking to others in a way that is perfectly agreeable and yet somehow makes it clear that there are certain distinctions" (*NNA,* 13). She is also the first to perceive their limitations as artists. It is she who makes the comment, cited earlier, about the lack of vision in Paula's sculptures and she who notes the narcissism and mediocrity of Greg's poems: "They are all about Greg. . . . poetry ought to make you look at things differently, whether it be feelings or the world or an idea or whatever. It should open things up. Greg's . . . is clamped inside his own head" (*NNA,* 30).

Lively involves Mary in a number of scenes and conversations that give her occasion to express the author's values, particularly those concerning art and artists. Mary is one of the few among both faculty and students who is interested in art rather than in the image of being an artist. Throughout the week, while most of the course members are busy ingratiating themselves with the staff and while the latter are busy shoring up their egos, Mary is assiduously at work producing art: she creates some truly good sketches and watercolors and is the only one who actually has something to show for her week at Framleigh. Believing in the importance of art and artists to society, she is increasingly distressed by the attitude of the Framleigh artists, such as the way they apparently feel that "not taking notice of other people is a necessary part of being an artist" (*NNA,* 100). She herself holds that, on the contrary, artists should "behave better than other people rather than the same or worse. If there's any truth in the idea that artists are different— that they are capable of things the rest of us aren't capable of, in seeing and understanding and being able to make other people see and understand" (*NNA,* 109). These sentiments are very much Lively's own, she having frequently expressed her repugnance for flamboyant artists like Dylan Thomas who consider themselves above rules of etiquette and her admiration for decent, modest artists like poet Philip Larkin.[3] (Significantly, when nonpretentious Nick mentions his liking of Larkin, his remark is met with a hoot of derision by Greg.)

Mary's views receive support when the featured guest novelist, Richard Waterton, gives a reading at Framleigh. Waterton is a serious, intellectual writer with a small following, not the kind of splashy big-name artist most of the course members and faculty would have preferred (but whom Toby, always doing things on the cheap, does not want to pay for). Not surprisingly, Mary is the only one who has read any of his works; Toby finds them too "heavy going" (*NNA,* 64). (Toby's true attitude toward art and ideas is also suggested by his library, which Mary finds "a disappointment, lined with row upon row of mainly empty shelves." The narrator explains, "Toby has sold off, over the years, any book to which value had accrued by virtue of age or rarity" [*NNA,* 56]). Waterton can barely conceal his disgust with the narcissism and self-centeredness of the staff, and he takes issue with the opinion voiced by Toby and Greg that the artist requires social detachment, asserting, "I must say I prefer involvement myself. Both for creative purposes and as an artistic responsibility" (*NNA,* 69).

Mary and Waterton also share, with each other as well as with Lively, a sincere interest in nature. Whereas most of the staff and course members are attracted to the contrived effects of Framleigh's grounds—its picturesquely arranged grottoes and rills and cascades—Mary is attracted to its authentically natural aspects. She goes off on long exploratory nature walks, getting down on her hands and knees to examine the local flora and fauna, while the others prefer to gaze from the terrace at the grounds' stylized views and vistas. She is delighted when she finds in Waterton a kindred spirit, and gratified when he confirms her hunch that a type of plant growing on the terrace is an erigeron daisy ("she and Waterton exchange looks of approval" [NNA, 65]). The Framleigh staff's obliviousness to nature is suggested by Paula's response to Waterton and Mary's discovery: "But it's a weed, surely?" Waterton's reply subtly but effectively exposes her ignorance and snobbishness: "'Even weeds,' says Waterton with a smile, 'have names' " (NNA, 65).

As the week wears on and the Framleigh staff's behavior increasingly offends Mary's values and moral principles, the normally quiet-spoken woman is driven to express her criticism. During the penultimate day's outing she becomes so exasperated with their attitude that she longs to cry out, like Carroll's Alice and like the protagonist of Lively's story of this title, "You're nothing but a pack of cards!" (NNA, 161). But she controls herself and instead begins to challenge Greg's and Paula's authoritative statements about art and artists—something no course member has dared before ("Paula is quite genuinely surprised to be confronted with a display of temperament in one who is just an ordinary person" [NNA, 161]). Although the Framleigh artists occasionally border on being caricatures, they are real enough that we receive a thrill of vindication when Mary, able to bear her irritation no longer, finally interrupts the insufferable Greg with the command, "Oh, be quiet!" (NNA, 161).

Lively's values—particularly her appreciation of nature and naturalness and her contempt for pretentiousness, exploitation, and dishonesty—are implied to one degree or another in all her fiction. But in this novel, as in her satiric short stories, they are the most forcefully asserted.

Nature, Art, and the Picturesque

The major target of Lively's criticism in Next to Nature, Art is people, artists in particular, who value image and style—or art—over nature and substance. The novel's title is an ironic allusion to a short, epitaph-like poem by Walter Savage Landor entitled "Finis," in which the speaker claims to have loved nature above all else "and next to Nature, Art." The irony is that the type of people Lively satirizes in her novel of this title are in fact more in love with art than with nature.

A major way Lively expresses her views on this topic is through her use of the eighteenth-century concept of the picturesque. One of the major forms this interest in the picturesque took was the contriving of artlessly natural, even wild, effects in landscaping and gardening. As one of Framleigh's more sophisticated course members explains in a discussion about picturesque landscaping, "It's the cult of the irregular, you see. And the natural. But the point is that the whole thing has to make a picture. You compose nature into a picture" (*NNA,* 41). Attention to the picturesque pervades the novel, in good part because of its setting. The Framleigh estate, built in 1740 when this fashion was at its height, was designed by the prominent eighteenth-century landscape architect William Kent and is "the perfect manifestation of the picturesque: Hogarthian lines of beauty, sham ruins, cascade, grotto, the lot. Twenty-five acres in which the disordered was cunningly turned into a contrivance, in which the physical world was made an artistic product, in which nature became art" (*NNA,* 9). Although all art is of course to some degree stylized and artificial, the truly natural being by definition not art, picturesque art is more so than many other types. It is excessively concerned with image and effect, and hence the novel's picturesque setting is appropriate for a tale about people who prefer images to reality.

Lively continually exposes the way Framleigh's inhabitants contrive to give the impression of valuing the natural while in truth they do not. As we have already seen, Framleigh's actual natural life concerns them far less than its studied natural effects. Ironically, one of the nature trail tours Toby leads the group on is almost ruined by the intrusion of a bit of real nature: a putrid, decaying mushroom whose overwhelming stench causes many staff members to want to turn back. Furthermore, there are many holes in the "back-to-nature," earthy facade the Framleigh Centre presents to its prospective clients. As Mary Chambers notes, the "simple country meals promised in the brochure" (*NNA,* 25) actually consist of supermarket rather than homemade bread and processed rather than local cheese. And Paula, as we have seen, has no interest in the botanical identification of daisies, but she likes the earth-mother effect they create when worn in a chain around her neck and complemented with a "skirt of material that pretends to be patchwork" (*NNA,* 2).

The art-versus-nature theme is also aided by Lively's technique of drawing attention to the discrepancy between the idealized, pictorial aspect of a scene and its not-so-perfect realities. For example, the opening statement of the novel—"Landscape with figures" (NNA, 1)—seems to be describing a painting, but as the paragraph continues we discover, first, that it is describing an actual landscape and, eventually, that this landscape is far from picture-perfect: "But something is wrong. The prospect is a hayfield, the ha-ha smothered in brambles, the terrace shaggy with weeds, the parterre to the side of it blurred almost to invisibility. And, where the eye should be drawn to the cleft in the horizon there is now a road, so that the glint of cars interrupts and distracts. Every half hour or so an aircraft blasts diagonally across, taking off from the American air-base half a mile away" (NNA, 1). Similarly, although Paula in her long floaty dress reminds a newcomer to Framleigh of "portraits in the Royal Academy Summer Exhibition of pretty, flimsily dressed women just called 'Celia' or 'Clarissa.' Women quite unlike one's wife, or sisters, or the wives of one's friends. And the candid stares of girls in French Impressionist paintings and Edwardian postcards of actresses in enormous hats—gay, racy people set aside from real life" (NNA, 180), we who have witnessed her day-to-day behavior know that with her coarse language and irritable manner Paula is very much a real person. And again, although from a distance the sight of little Jason setting off across a sun-dappled meadow may "seem an image of idyllic childhood: a long ago photograph, a scene from the cinema of sensibility" (NNA, 24), the reality is that he's stealing away to smoke a cigarette lifted from one of the adult's pockets. Again and again Lively deflates the picturesque with the real and natural so as to suggest the image-consciousness of the Framleigh way of life.

Although in this novel Lively does not explicitly express her philosophy of art, she does reveal some of her attitudes in her treatment both of artists and of the concept of the picturesque. The preceding analysis is not meant to suggest that she is antiart; on the contrary, she believes that art serves the important purpose of imposing order and pattern on the chaos of reality.[4] Nor does she advocate a totally unmediated approach to nature; indeed, in many of her novels she suggests that such an approach is impossible, for we cannot perceive reality raw but must inevitably filter it through our mental cargo of images and allusions. The creating of and responding to images, Lively feels, is an important and desirable activity of the imagination. What she is against is the commercial exploitation of images and the use of them to distort reality—particularly to prettify it and make it picturesque. She sets up the Framleigh staff as examples of artists who engage in this kind of pernicious manipulation. We can thus infer from this novel Lively's belief that the artist should be a moral person and that art should reflect and illuminate, not distort, reality and nature. Like the speaker of the poem alluded to in the title, and unlike the artists she satirizes in this novel, Lively loves nature, and "next to nature, art."

Conclusion

Next to Nature, Art is not typical of Lively's long fiction. It lacks the compassionate exploration of character and the heavy emphasis on the past that readers have come to associate with her work. It does, however, demonstrate certain other tendencies: her flair for humor and comedy of manners; her skill at constructing crisp, telling dramatic scenes; and her use of satire to assert strongly held values and moral convictions. These are features that figure to one degree or another in all her fiction, but they are given their most complete expression in *Next to Nature, Art.*

Chapter Five

Perfect Happiness

After her foray into satire and comedy of manners in *Next to Nature, Art,* Lively returned in her fifth novel to her more typical novelistic territory. *Perfect Happiness* (1983), with its intelligent, observant female protagonist, its concern with the past, and its interweaving of memories and flashbacks into the narrative action, is quintessential Lively. Although, as observant readers no doubt notice, by her fifth novel Lively has become repetitive in some of her observations and phrasings (such as her reflections on the palimpsest quality of people and places and her figurative use of the words *tethered, hitched,* and *kaleidoscopic*), reviewers praised *Perfect Happiness* for its scrupulous representation of experience and for Lively's ability to plumb emotions without becoming sentimental or melodramatic. This novel, like most of Lively's others, is largely concerned with exploring states of mind. As one reviewer comments, "It is not, obviously, an exciting book, but it is a compelling one. . . . It is a novel which will extend and deepen the reader's understanding of how people behave."[1]

Plot, Characters, and Point of View

The protagonist is Frances Brooklyn, a 49-year-old woman who possesses many of the qualities of Anne Linton and Clare Paling and indeed of Lively herself. Frances is shrewdly intelligent but modest, and she is given to strong but understated emotions. Like Anne and Clare, she has lived a quietly conventional life, with her marriage and family the focus of her existence. When the novel opens Frances is struggling with the grief occasioned by the sudden death eight months earlier of her husband, Steven, a celebrated expert on international relations. The narrative follows her over the course of the ensuing summer and fall as she learns to cope with her loneliness and disorientation. But the process of healing is never a tidily progressive one, and Lively very accurately portrays the way grief "ebbs and flows in tides, . . . steals away to a distance and then comes roaring back."[2] Frances has moments of overwhelming emptiness and panic when she yearns to return to the past, but then her gritty determination reasserts itself and she resumes her efforts to create a new life. These efforts include selling her home and moving to an unfamiliar section of London, devoid of associations with Steven; beginning to form friendships entirely on her own; and, eventually, taking a permanent job as an editorial assistant. Incrementally, Frances gains strength and a sense of hopefulness as she discovers the satisfactions of these accomplishments.

Frances is also bolstered by a number of important relationships. Foremost among these is the one with Steven's sister, Zoe, with whom she has been close since college (it was Zoe who introduced Frances and Steven). Zoe is another familiar type of Lively female: the gutsy, crusty, nonmarrying career woman—she is a successful journalist—whose tough exterior masks a warm heart and passionate nature (*Treasures of Time*'s Aunt Nellie and *Moon Tiger*'s Claudia also exemplify this type). An intriguing fact of Zoe and Frances's relationship, which partly accounts for its extraordinary closeness, is that Zoe is actually the mother of Frances's 21-year-old adopted daughter, Tabitha. An accretion of elliptical flashbacks and oblique allusions leads us to suspect this fact, and it is finally confirmed by a fully developed flashback. We learn that Frances could not have children but desperately wanted them, so when Zoe accidentally became pregnant the two women hit upon the perfect solution and managed to talk Steven into it. The facts of Tabitha's adoption have been revealed to virtually no one else, not even to Tabitha (until the end of the novel). Frances also has another, more conventionally adopted child, Harry, who is a year younger than Tabitha. Like Anne, Clare, and a number of Lively's other women, Frances is deeply maternal, experiencing the same rushes of tenderness for her children that they do for theirs. Her relationship with Harry and Tab, then, is another source of strength for Frances, although the two are absent on summer holidays during much of the narrative.

Of her other nourishing relationships, one is with a 60-year-old American tourist named Ruth Bowers whom Frances meets when she is called suddenly to Venice to tend to Harry, who has been hurt in a terrorist bomb explosion while vacationing there. Venice is where she and Steven had honeymooned, and its associations cause Frances to become more distraught and disoriented than usual. Sensing her vulnerability, Ruth takes her under her wing, and the older woman's sensible, optimistic attitude and homely wisdom are just the antidote Frances needs. Their friendship develops during this time in Venice and continues even after the two return to their respective countries, with Ruth paying

Frances a visit in London later in the fall. For Frances, Ruth becomes an inspiration and a beacon of hope, a reminder that it is the little ordinary acts of human kindness and decency that make life meaningful.

Patricia Geering, the editor of the academic journal Frances eventually accepts a job with, serves much the same purpose in the latter's psychological recovery. Like Ruth, Patricia is the kind of ordinary, down-to-earth person Steven tended to steer away from, being more attracted to those with intellectual verve. In fact, Steven had known Patricia, whose journal is sponsored by the think-tank institute he was affiliated with, and had found her uninteresting. But Frances discovers in this unassuming woman the same valuable, life-affirming qualities she found in Ruth Bowers: both women have carved meaningful, fulfilling lives out of meager resources (they are plain-looking, middle-aged spinsters), and both are capable of steady, loyal friendship. Patricia too becomes a buoy and a source of inspiration for Frances.

Yet another significant relationship Frances develops is with Morris Corfield, a middle-aged musicologist and friend of Zoe, who introduces the two. Like Ruth and Patricia, Morris leads a quiet, solitary life (his wife left him years ago), and he, too, is a kindly, decent person capable of strong attachment. He and Frances fall into an easy companionship, which eventually takes on sexual overtones as Morris becomes increasingly attracted to Frances and fancies himself in love with her. Although Frances feels no more than a warm affection for him and continues to miss her husband terribly, she does ultimately make love with Morris, having found herself in a state of increasing sexual tension since Steven's death. At the novel's end the future of the relationship is up in the air, but it is clear that Morris, like Ruth and Patricia, has contributed to the gradual return of happiness and hopefulness in Frances's life.

As the above sketch suggests, this is a quiet, somewhat static novel, concerned mainly with portraying the power of friendship and human connection. What action there is is psychological—Frances's gradual overcoming of despair. But, like Lively's other novels, it is also wryly humorous in places and possesses a richly textured, "felt life" quality. As one reviewer observes, "The whole thing could have become solemn and plangent; but without shifting attention from Frances's grief and her attempts to cure the 'chronic illness' which it is, the book takes in so much else, and with such circumstantial subtlety, that the quirks of private sufferings and the little absurdities of daily lives are made an essential part of the fabric."[3] There are, for example, some wonderfully comic scenes in which Frances, unfamiliar with the ways of dogs, tries to cope with the lovable but headstrong puppy her son gives her (one of Lively's strengths, as has been pointed out before, is her humorous, realistic portrayal of the behavior of dogs). There are bits of stringent social satire, as when Frances attends a cocktail party and finds herself trapped in conversation with an insensitive, nosy social climber. And there is a very realistically presented account of Frances's awkward, reluctant involvement with a raffish bohemian couple down the street who pour out their marital problems to her. As always, Lively manages to paint a vivid picture of her characters' quotidian existences with precise, deftly rendered details.

Lively employs her usual roving third-person limited narrative approach in this novel, shifting among the points of view of the main characters and frequently repeating the same episode two or three times in kaleidoscopic fashion. The effect of this technique here, though, is not so much to emphasize the subjective nature of perception as to reveal the deeply private nature of human beings' emotional lives. In these third-person glimpses we learn not only of Frances's midnight struggles with loneliness but of Zoe's terror as she faces alone the threat of cancer, of Tabitha's internal anguish over the dissolution of her first love affair, and of Morris's bouts with self-doubt as he embarks on his first romance since his wife rejected him. Like *Judgment Day,* which this novel resembles in many ways, *Perfect Happiness* presents an intimate and compassionate portrayal of the characters' emotional lives.

The Potency and Distortion of Memory

Like most of Lively's other main characters, Frances and Zoe are sensitive to the palimpsest quality of place, detecting reverberations of the past in contemporary surroundings. In the opening scene, for example, Zoe, sitting in a Cambridge concert hall listening to Tabitha perform in a student orchestra recital, gazes at the ancient portraits on the walls and reflects on the ghosts of people of previous generations that fill the room: "Once careful hands created the plasterwork of that ceiling. Other eyes have blinked in the light from that window. Through this room have passed beliefs too alien to contemplate" (*PH,* 1–2). Frances has a similar insight a few pages later: passing by a graveyard on her way to a luncheon engagement, she suddenly stops, paralyzed by the vision of these "marshalled dead," this "silent army in the sour London soil" (*PH,* 17).

Both women are also hyperaware of the ghosts of their own personal pasts hovering around them. Struggling to keep her emotional equilibrium, Frances, for example, feels much of the time as if she is walking through minefields, for so many of the places where she finds herself hold painful associations with Steven. And both women are prone to Proustian memory plunges triggered by chance stimuli. Indeed, as in many of Lively's other novels, in *Perfect Happiness* the main narrative is continually interrupted by such flashbacks. The effect of these here, as elsewhere, is to demonstrate both the extent to which our pasts preoccupy us and the seamless way our minds move between absorption in memory and consciousness of the present.

A major point Lively makes in this novel is that our memories are inevitably subjective and partial. Employing the same kind of plot device she did in *The Road to Lichfield,* she has Frances, like Anne, unearth a piece of evidence that alters her understanding of the past and hence disorients her: on her obligatory monthly visit to her mother-in-law, Frances discovers in an old photo album a snapshot of Steven, taken a few years before she met him, with a young woman whom, Mrs. Brooklyn explains, he was briefly engaged to. Frances has been ignorant of this episode in his life and the discovery jolts her, making her realize how tenuous her interpretation of the past is. Using one of Lively's characteristic metaphors, she thinks, "The kaleidoscope was twisted, the pattern of the past re-assembled" (*PH,* 164) and "Everything—each day, each moment—had to be adjusted to accommodate the distant shadowy figure of this girl" (*PH,* 166).

The impossibility of seeing the past clearly, according to Lively, is caused not only by the partial nature of evidence but also by the fact that our recollection of an event is influenced by all that has occurred subsequent to it: its "resonances are always the same and yet also subtly different, charged with the insights of today, and yesterday" (*PH,* 2). The complexity of this mental phenomenon is mused on by Frances when, looking through her wedding album, she realizes that her memory of her wedding day is an amalgam of the expectations she recalls having had prior to the day, the day itself, the honeymoon, and all that has happened since then. Further, this memory is "susceptible of course to the revisions of what is yet to be" (*PH,* 27). Thus, just as it is impossible to know exactly how earlier cultures experienced reality—a point Lively makes in other novels—so is it impossible to recall exactly how we thought and felt when experiencing an episode in our own personal past.

One way we distort the past that Lively particularly explores in this novel is to intensify the happiness we recall having felt during certain experiences. The novel's title is an allusion to those moments of "perfect happiness" that lodge in our memory and become more emotionally loaded as time goes by. But the undiluted bliss of these experiences exists almost exclusively in hindsight; as Frances observes, "We are never happy now, only then" (*PH,* 7). When we are actually experiencing these episodes, our emotions are usually mixed and our attention dispersed. But with repeated recollection the extraneous emotions and details fade away, and the moment is crystallized into one of anadulterated happiness.

Frances has several such idealized memories, in which the episode recalled seems to have been flooded with an almost symbolic light and shot through with significance. For example, she is from time to time arrested by the memory of a particular "summer afternoon, with sunshine falling onto the lawn through the branches of the apple tree to lie like gold pennies among the daisies. Idyllic, unreachable summer afternoon" (*PH,* 116), with Steven and herself reading on the lawn, the children gamboling about, and Zoe suddenly arriving, "sweeping in with laughter and parcels and traveller's tales. The afternoon softens to evening, but it will never end, they will all be there for ever on the lavish grass in the sunshine" (*PH,* 117). Although distortions, these golden, finely chiseled moments are, as we shall see, a source of great strength for Frances.

As in her other novels, Lively's demonstration in *Perfect Happiness* of the potency of memory suggests that time is as much a subjective, psychological phenomenon as it is an objective, linear one. Her characters tend to be very aware of this; Tab, for example, reflects that "time is not only to do with months or weeks, it is to do with feelings and what you know and who you are" (*PH,* 193). The most extreme demonstration of the power of subjective time is Frances's delusion in Venice that she is actually reentering the time of her honeymoon by returning to the spots she and Steven visited: "The past lost all chronology; its jumbled fragments came and went with kaleidoscopic brilliance" (*PH,* 57). This mental reliving of potent past experiences is common in Lively's novels, but Frances has taken it too far and stepped over the boundary between memory and delusion, actually believing for a while that she can crash through the constraints of linear time.

Mercifully, this near mental breakdown is short-lived. With the help of Ruth Bowers, Frances is able to regain her grip on reality, and she begins to make an effort to diminish the hold the past has on her, developing friendships and interests unrelated to Steven. This is not to say that she turns her back on the past completely; those blissful sunlit memories continue to have a powerful hold on her, but she begins to notice the sunlit moments of her present life as well. Toward the end of the novel, "on a morning in early October, she came downstairs through her house and was pleased with what she saw. She drew back the curtains in the sitting room and early sun flooded in" (*PH,* 195), and she suddenly realizes the progress she has made. Then in a gesture symbolizing her belief in the future, she walks out into the backyard and begins to make plans for next summer's garden.

What Lively seems to be suggesting in her chronicle of Frances's gradual relinquishing of the past and her struggle to stay linked to linear time is the need for a balance between past and present in one's personal life. Memory is important—as distorted and subjective as it inevitably is, it provides us with a sense of identity and continuity—but an obsession with the past, to the extent that Frances takes it of losing the ability to distinguish between chronological and mental time, is unhealthy. This is the same point Lively makes about the historical past in *The Road to Lichfield* and other novels: advocacy of historic preservation at all costs and the assumption that the past is superior to the present are misguided attitudes. A healthy balance between past and present, in both the public and the private arenas, is what Lively urges. She expresses this idea through Frances at the end of the novel: "I must not, she thought with sudden clarity, be forever hitched to what has been. Only to such of it as I choose, to such of it that will sustain me" (*PH,* 225).

The Feminist Subtext

Although by no means a major, and perhaps not even a conscious, theme, there is indisputably a feminist subtext in this novel. Lively, as we know, does not identify herself as a feminist writer, and her major themes are not concerned with exclusively female issues. Nonetheless, *Perfect Happiness* does invite a feminist reading, and it is surprising that the book has thus far not been mined by feminist critics.

Although Frances never analyzes it in these terms, her recovery is as much a movement from an unliberated to a liberated condition as it is a movement from the past into the present. Prior to Steven's death, she lived a very traditional female life, with her marriage the center of her existence: "she thought of [her husband] for much of every day; his moods and his requirements dominated her life not by reason of selfishness or arrogance but because she wished it so. He was her centre" (*PH,* 31). For Steven, on the other hand, the marriage was a thing apart: he loved his wife and was faithful to her, but his career was clearly primary and his mind occupied much of the time with concerns other than Frances.

With Steven gone, though, Frances is forced to act on her own, and in doing so she finds herself, to her own surprise, forming opinions contrary to what she assumes Steven's would have been, not out of any perversity or sense of rebellion but because she is learning to heed her own voice. The first time she realizes she is doing this is toward the end of her stay in Venice, when she notes the "flow of warmth she had felt for Ruth Bowers, a stranger, and the faint but inescapable satisfaction that she was alone in this encounter. Steven would not have cared for Ruth Bowers. Steven would have found Ruth Bowers tedious and uninteresting. Which she is not, Frances thought. Which *I think* she is not" (*PH*, 71; emphasis added). She has a similar flash of insight the first day she goes to work for Patricia Geering: "She was a kind, decent woman, assiduous about her work. Steven had dismissed her as tiresome. He was wrong, Frances thought. I accepted, too readily, his opinion of people" (*PH*, 148). And she even forms her own opinion about dogs: when her son presents her with a puppy, she is about to decline his gift, claiming she's never had a dog and is not sure whether she likes them, until Harry points out to her that the reason they'd never had one is "because Dad didn't like them" (*PH*, 90). Frances immediately changes her mind and accepts the puppy.

Very gradually, then, Frances is gaining autonomy and separating her identity from Steven. In the process, it is implied, she is also coming to alter her view of him. As we know, Lively is interested in the question of the partial nature of evidence and addresses this issue in most of her novels, usually by means of her multiple-points-of-view approach. Here she does so by causing the reader to piece together a different picture of Steven from the one Frances herself has had of him throughout their marriage. The reader garners evidence from Frances's recollections and from other characters' comments about Steven, and thereby infers that he had many shortcomings that Frances, whose interpretation has been colored by wifely adoration, does not perceive: he lacked passion (Frances reflects that it was she "who knew rapture" whereas "Steven was good at sex like he was good at everything but he could manage quite happily without it and he was never for one instant, I suspect, lost in it" [*PH*, 10]); he was impatient with those who weren't as bright as he; he valued intellect over such other important human qualities as kindness and goodness; and he lacked imagination (Frances recalls attempting to share with him her astonishment at the mysterious way our lives intersect with those of strangers: "She saw now his expression, at once puzzled and slightly impatient. He had not understood her; it was not the kind of thing about which he thought, it did not interest him. He . . . found the idea sterile" [*PH*, 82]).

Although Frances never reaches the point where she thinks she was altogether wrong in her view of Steven, she is presumably beginning to see him differently as she acquires evidence that conflicts with her former view—such as the evidence that Patricia Geering is an interesting person and that Steven's not finding her so implies a limitation on his part. Frances's altered attitude is reflected in her increasing annoyance with those who continue to idolize Steven. Visiting with her mother-in-law, for example, she becomes quietly enraged by the woman's habit of continually deflecting the conversation from the topic of Zoe's career success back to Steven's. And at the cocktail party celebrating the launching of a memorial lecture series in Steven's name, Frances endures "with mounting resentment" the obsessive talk about Steven and "wished she hadn't come" (*PH*, 225). It is with great relief that, upon arriving home that night, she receives a surprise visit from Ruth Bowers, who symbolizes Frances's new, post-Steven life.

Feminist readers of Lively's work who were annoyed that the author did not have Anne Linton, in *The Road to Lichfield*, follow through on her misgivings about her marriage to oppressive Don (who, incidentally, bears a striking resemblance to Steven in his lack of passion and imagination) are no doubt satisfied with the way she allows Frances to develop. In a sense, Anne and Frances are paving the way for the fullest expression of Lively's feminist impulse, which will take the form of the radically unconventional Claudia Hampton in *Moon Tiger*.

The Anxiety of Agnosticism

Penelope Lively's philosophical outlook is very much a modern agnostic one. Virtually all of her protagonists and main characters share her agnosticism as well as the peculiar anxiety it gives rise to. Lively has mentioned experiencing an occasional longing for the kind of certainty that religious faith provides,[4] and some of her characters from time to time voice this same longing (Zoe, Frances, and Tabitha, for example [*PH*, 158]). The anxiety of agnosticism pervades her novels—some, such as *Perfect Happiness,* more than others—and reveals itself in a number of different ways.

One such way is her characters' hyperawareness of the essential chaos and meaninglessness of the universe. Characters are made very uneasy by the dizzying sensation this awareness creates and hence continually try to latch onto solid certainties. One of these certainties is the dependability of particular people in one's life; Frances, for example, serves this purpose for Zoe, being her "still calm centre" (*PH,* 6, 13). Another certainty is physical reality. Lively's characters often reflect on the role physical objects and places play in maintaining their sanity and sense of structure; as Frances observes, these things take on "the quality of anchors" (*PH,* 196). Yet another anchor is clock, or chronological, time. And for some characters, such as *Judgment Day*'s Clare Paling, it is language, which imposes structure and meaning on reality, that serves as their anchor.[5]

But Lively's characters can easily lose their grip and find themselves feeling untethered from these certainties, "only tenuously connected to the physical world" (*PH,* 18). It is this condition that overwhelms Frances in Venice, when, worn down by grief and exhaustion, she cannot maintain her grasp on chronological time and feels adrift in "a continuous present" (*PH,* 51). This is simply an extreme, pathological version of the state of mind most of Lively's characters incline toward. *Judgment Day*'s Martin Bryan, for example, is prone to feeling lost in time and space and must reanchor himself by reciting the reassuring litany, cited earlier, "Martin Keith Bryan, aged ten, 3 The Green, Laddenham, nr. Spelbury, Oxfordshire, England, Europe, The World, the Universe" (*JD,* 31).

Zoe experiences something akin to Martin's sensation when, flying over the Atlantic, she gazes out the window and queasily reflects on the dizzying expanse of space surrounding the plane. This prompts her to remark to a fellow passenger, "If people in aircraft stopped to think where they were you'd have a riot on your hands. . . . Mind, that could be said of life in general, I suppose" (*PH,* 13). Like Frances, Zoe easily loses her grip on chronological time during such vulnerable moments. Spending the day in the hospital prior to her biopsy, for example, she feels cut loose from the laws of physical reality: "The day folded back and forth; she was no longer in real time, just as she was no longer in the real world" (*PH,* 188). Like Martin, she knows that to reanchor herself she must immerse herself in facts about the physical world: "That's the kind of thing that keeps people sane, she thought, at rough moments. Constancy. That night will follow day. That the world at least is reliable" (*PH,* 79).

Lively's characters thus take comfort in the dependability and continuity of the physical world; but they are also keenly aware of, and disturbed by, its indifference to human beings. This uneasy awareness is
another reflection of their agnostic anxiety. Lively herself has remarked
on, and has several of her characters remark on, how odd it is that the
physical world can be so movingly beautiful and yet so utterly meaningless and indifferent.[6] Frances, for example, reflects that such "beauty is
constant, heartless and quite detached from the beholder" (*PH,* 127),
and Zoe, gazing out a London bus window at "the symmetries of the
darkly stooping trees in the parks, the opalescence of clouds above the
river," is transfixed by the beauty of the world but at the same time
struck by "its indifference" (*PH,* 187). The frequency with which this
type of observation appears in Lively's fiction seems to betray a wistful
yearning on both author's and characters' parts for some kind of metaphysical significance or God-like intelligence behind physical reality.

Despite their acknowledgment of the insentience and aloofness of the
physical world, Lively's characters indulge frequently in the pathetic fal-
lacy. As we have seen, in their memories they often project the emotions
they experienced during a particular episode onto the setting of that
episode, and hence a tree, a bowl of flowers, or a sun-dappled lawn
seems in recollection to shimmer with significance. But they are fully
aware that their own minds are projecting this significance. In fact,
Lively's characters come close to embracing the philosophy of solipsism,
for they tend to believe that reality is inherently meaningless and that it
is only the individual perceiver's mind that endows it with significance
and structure. In this they again reveal their agnosticism, their inability
to believe that a supreme being presides over reality and imbues it with
meaning.

Lively's own tendency toward solipsism is suggested by her belief in
the subjective nature of evidence, reflected in her characteristic multiple-
points-of-view technique, and by her demonstration of the power of subjective time in her characters' consciousnesses. And her characters in turn
reveal their solipsism in their tendency to suspect that reality exists only
inside one's head. Usually they are just bemused by this idea, as is
Tabitha when she rides a bus through the London streets and is struck by
how "extraordinary [it is] that she and [all the other passengers] should
look out onto the same streets and buildings, locked each into private
visions" (*PH,* 183). But in vulnerable moments such insights make them
anxious, and they long for certainties and absolutes. For example,
Frances, distraught by grief, panics when she realizes that the loss of

Steven makes their past together less real because one of the minds that contained it has vanished. "I have this odd feeling these days that absolutely nothing is real," she says to Zoe. "Not even the past. Especially the past. I can't really explain what it's like. It's as though because Steven is no longer here there is nothing to confirm what happened when he was. How we were together" (*PH*, 19–20). She fears "that if she ceased for one moment to think about Steven, to carry him with her in her head, she might lose him. He was dead; he existed only in recollection; when recollection ceased even that tenuous existence would be gone" (*PH*, 57).

Of all Lively's protagonists, Frances is the most prone to such doubts about objective reality. But again, hers is simply an extreme version of the same mental condition toward which most of Lively's characters are inclined. Like their author, they are agnostics who are both preoccupied with and made uneasy by the tenuous nature of reality and the absence of metaphysical certainties.

Affirmation, Epiphanies, and the Influence of Woolf and Forster

Given the anxieties the author and the characters are prone to, one might expect Lively's fictional world to be a bleak, nihilistic place, with characters groping for a metaphysical meaning and structure that continually eludes them. But on the contrary, Lively's is a hopeful, life-affirming vision. Despite their propensity for feelings of panic and emptiness, her characters for the most part find life to be "pretty damn good" (*PH*, 185), to quote Zoe. What gives it beauty and meaning are those quasimystical moments that descend almost like visitations of grace, as well as the ability to connect with other human beings.

Perfect Happiness, like *Judgment Day,* presents a number of such redeeming moments: those experiences of "perfect happiness" described earlier. These are moments that seem to exist outside "the straitjacket of time" (*PH*, 50), "fragments and passages from days which are of another order altogether. They are beyond and without chronology; they hang suspended, possessions for all time. To be called up out of darkness" (*PH*, 85). They become lodged in one's consciousness and mentally recur and reverberate down through the years, accruing increasing luminosity and clarity as they do so. Thus, although such a moment has occurred in the past, it takes on its beauty and significance only through the process of memory, and hence it continues to uplift one long after it first took place.

Lively portrays the crystallized memories these experiences are trans-formed into—those light-filled, iconic scenarios Frances recalls—as well as some such experiences in the making. The novel begins with one of the latter. Zoe and Frances are at Cambridge listening to Tabitha play violin in a student performance of the fifth Brandenburg concerto; Zoe's old friend Morris Corfield also turns out to be there, listening to his son perform, and Zoe introduces Morris to Frances. Although none of the characters is aware of it at the time, this experience, we are informed by the narrator (who is omniscient at the outset and then dissolves into rov-ing limited third person), "is for one of them, for two, perhaps for sever-al, a moment outside time, one of those moments when the needle gets stuck, when what happens goes on happening down the years, again and again, recorded messages of glassy clarity" (*PH,* 2). And sure enough, as the narrative develops, we see how this memory reverberates in the minds of Zoe, Frances, and Morris, and how over time it becomes more sharply etched and more imbued with significance, reduced to a few selective, emotionally charged details: the strains of the Brandenburg fifth concerto; the portraits on the wall; Tab's seriously concentrating face above her frilly white shirt (for Zoe, who was transfixed by pride and emotion); Frances's sad, lovely face (for Morris, who would eventu-ally fall in love with her). There are a handful of other such moments in the making—Morris's catching Frances's eye across the room at a dinner party and feeling suddenly filled with wild happiness, Zoe's listening to a ward nurse's miraculous yet matter-of-fact announcement that her tumor has turned out to be benign, Frances's walking into her sunlit liv-ing room and suddenly realizing her life is going to be all right. With each of these, we can envision the way it will be transformed by memory into one of those "brilliant tethered moments" (*PH,* 17) that stay lodged in the characters' minds and continue to illuminate their lives.

Lively describes these luminous moments in almost religious terms, and in their transcendence they do somewhat resemble religious experi-ences. But the crucial difference is that Lively does not believe in God and that the moments she portrays are not divinely sent. Rather, they are supreme acts of the imagination: it is the imagination of the individ-ual experiencing and recollecting these moments that imbues them with their significance. They are thus closer to those Joycean or Woolfian flashes of clarity sometimes called epiphanies than they are to traditional mystic experiences. In fact, one is frequently reminded of Virginia Woolf, particularly of her *Mrs. Dalloway,* when reading *Perfect Happiness.* Although Lively does not cite Woolf as an influence, the sensibilities of the two writers are similar in many ways. Like Clarissa Dalloway and other Woolf characters, Frances and Zoe range between feelings of anxiety over the emptiness and meaninglessness of existence and sudden high moments of transcendent joy when they are struck by the sheer richness and beauty of life and when the physical world seems unusually alive and sentient. In both novels there are scenes in which a character rides or strolls through the London streets noting the palpable quality of the atmosphere and reflecting on the waves of humanity that have washed through these streets and left something of themselves there (the desultory afternoon Tabitha spends riding buses around London is very reminiscent of a similar afternoon spent by young Elizabeth Dalloway). This connection between Woolf and Lively will be explored more extensively in the discussion of *City of the Mind,* the novel that shows the strongest influence of Woolf and *Mrs. Dalloway.*

One can also perceive in *Perfect Happiness* the influence of another Bloomsbury writer, E. M. Forster. Indeed, the novel's opening scene is reminiscent of the famous chapter 5 of *Howards End,* in which most of the main characters are congregated at a musical performance—only here it is Beethoven's fifth rather than Bach's—and we are given glimpses into their private thoughts as they listen to the orchestra.[7] Lively may not have had this scene consciously in mind when she constructed her opening, but certainly she does make a conscious allusion to *Howards End* when she describes Zoe's career as involving her in the "world of telegrams and not anger" (*PH,* 6)—a clever variation of the phrase "the world of telegrams and anger" that serves as something of a refrain throughout Forster's book and signifies the philistine, bullying life-style of people like the Wilcoxes as opposed to the life of ideas and art of people like the Schlegels. But it is *Howards End*'s vision of the possibilities of human connection—expressed in its epigraph "Only connect"—that is its most important influence on *Perfect Happiness.* As does Forester in that book, Lively here celebrates such connections. She shows that it is friendship and human kindness, as well as the luminous moments that lurk in one's memory, that keep at bay her characters' agnostic anxieties.

The central friendship portrayed in the novel is Zoe and Frances's. It serves as an anchor for both, tethering them to reality and to sanity. Zoe reflects on its importance: "I've known Frances all my adult life. For twenty-five years she has been there. Friendship is the love that is ignored; people

don't theorise about friendship, write poetry about it. It just goes quietly along, sustaining. Passion spends itself . . . but friendship is always
there. . . . the feeling for Frances is constant, permanent" (*PH,* 76). Such
quietly sustaining friendships are what make life bearable and beautiful
for Lively's characters. As we have seen, in addition to her friendship
with Zoe, the relationships Frances forms with Ruth Bowers, Patricia
Geering, and Morris Corfield save her from panic and insanity and offer
her a life-affirming vision of the future. This vision involves an insight
into the importance of simple acts of human kindness—such as Ruth's
sensing her vulnerability in Venice and going out of her way to support
her, and Patricia's intuiting her need for occupation and routine and
accordingly creating a job for her. These gestures of friendship are made
in a quiet, understated way, and yet there is something miraculous and
heroic about them. Frances articulates this point when she suddenly
grasps the value of a person like Ruth Bowers: "This is a good woman,
Frances thought, you expect goodness to go around with some sort of
distinguishing mark—uniforms and robes and discreet medals—but
when it turns up it is decked with apricot crimplene and an ugly jockey
cap and gilt-framed sunglasses" (*PH,* 69). And, indeed, the other emis-
saries of kindness in Frances's life come in equally ordinary, even dowdy,
guises: Patricia has bad teeth and lives a spinsterish existence; Morris is
dumpy looking and considers himself unexciting. But the contribution
of such people to life's richness is far from ordinary. As one reviewer
sums up, "Kindness is a virtue hardly celebrated in contemporary fiction.
Mrs. Lively does it justice" (Massie, 5).

   The novel ends on a note of affirmation, with Frances in the quietly
hopeful mood that has gradually overtaken her during the preceding
months. In fact, she is experiencing one of those moments that will no
doubt eventually be crystallized and illuminated by memory. Driving
home through London traffic after spending the afternoon with Zoe and
Tabitha at Cambridge, she is flooded with an almost visionary awareness
of the beauty of the evening, projecting her newfound hopefulness onto
the inanimate world: "She thought it beautiful, and was quietly exhilarated, as though this were some private vision. She drove towards her
house, neither happy nor grieving, looking not backwards into the day
but on into the next" (*PH,* 234). One can imagine the way the brilliant
jewellike lights that are the predominant feature of this scene will contribute to the luminous quality the memory will acquire over time.
Although Frances will undoubtedly have periods in the future when she
once again teeters on the edge of the abyss, she will always be able to

summon up moments such as this, or turn to one of her quietly sustaining friendships, and thereby banish her existential angst.

Conclusion

If *Next to Nature, Art* gives the fullest expression of the crisp, satiric side of Lively, *Perfect Happiness* does the same for her romantic, visionary side. Although it contains satiric, comic elements and is generally written in Lively's characteristic compressed style, what lingers in the reader's mind after finishing the book is the luminous, Woolfian quality of those scenes portraying moments of epiphany and of human connection. Thus, by this point in her writing career Lively had demonstrated the complexity and range of her sensibility. Taken as a whole, her first five novels reveal that she shares with Austen and the eighteenth century an amused, sardonic view of humanity, a strong moral streak, and an interest in nature, art, and the picturesque; with George Eliot, Thomas Hardy, and the Victorians a compassionate attitude toward human beings' struggles against life's misfortunes and vagaries; with Woolf, Forster, and the modernists an interest in secular epiphanies and in experimental narrative techniques; and with her own times an agnostic outlook and an awareness that there is no absolute reality.

Chapter Six
According to Mark

According to Mark (1984), like most of Lively's other books, combines the qualities of an entertaining social satire with those of a novel of ideas. Shortlisted for the Booker Prize, it was praised by most reviewers, who commented on its wit, its deft depiction of character and incident, and its clever treatment of the theme alluded to in the title: the idea that there is no definitive version of a person's life. A few reviewers, however, noted shortcomings, namely a somewhat clichéd plot, some unrealistic situations, and a certain lack of passion. These flaws, which most reviewers characterized as detracting in only a minor way from the novel's overall effectiveness, are probably the result of Lively's concentrating too heavily in places on ideas or comedy of manners and not enough on realism.

Lightly satirical in mood (one reviewer calls it a "martini-dry" comedy of manners),[1] this book, somewhat like *Next to Nature, Art,* does not probe characters' thoughts and feelings in the kind of sympathetic depth that most of Lively's novels do. The narrative unfolds in the author's usual fashion, with the point of view shifting among the main characters, but rather than portray the raw, private contents of their minds, Lively filters their thoughts through the dry, wry voice of an omniscient narrator, who also provides background information on the characters. It is a more conventional approach than she usually employs; little of her characteristic kaleidoscopic technique is present. Although a major concern of the novel is the partial, subjective nature of evidence, this theme is conveyed not so much via narrative technique as via plot and situation.

The Plot

The kernel for the plot of *According to Mark* appears to have been the short story entitled "The Art of Biography," which Lively published three years earlier. Like the protagonist of that work, Mark Lamming is a scholarly biographer whose research into the personal life and loves of his deceased subject takes on the quality of a detective tale as he encounters conflicting and puzzling evidence and becomes obsessed with making sense of it. Another forerunner of Mark in Lively's oeuvre is *Treasures of*

Time's Tom Rider, who, like Mark, tries to step imaginatively into the mind of his subject and experience the world the way he did. Mark's subject is the late Gilbert Strong, an Edwardian man of letters (essayist, novelist, playwright, biographer) who hobnobbed with Wells, Galsworthy, and Shaw and who was on the fringes of the Bloomsbury group but whose name and works have faded in the public's memory.

The novel takes place during an approximate six-month period when Mark is completing the research phase of his project. As it opens he has just received permission from the trustees of Strong's estate to pay a visit to Dean Close, Strong's rural home in Dorset, and go through whatever pertinent materials are housed there. The discovery at Dean Close of a hitherto unknown cache of letters, as well as of Strong's 32-year-old granddaughter, Carrie Summers, who lives in the house and operates a commercial garden center on its grounds, gives rise to the novel's two major plot strands.

The Research Plot Strand

Provocative gaps in Strong's correspondence launch Mark onto a kind of literary sleuthing adventure in which he tries to solve the puzzle of where the man was and whom he was with during certain unaccounted for periods.[2] Mark is prone to fascinating insights about the relationship a biographer develops with his deceased subject, how it cuts across the boundaries of time and proceeds along the same lines of increasing intimacy as does a relationship between two living persons. Mark discovers that Strong is a far more complex character than he had at first thought: his sleuthwork unearths evidence of a passionate, doomed love affair that Strong apparently wanted to hide from posterity, for this vulnerable, emotional side of himself conflicted with the Hemingwayesque image he increasingly projected as he grew older and went through two marriages and several extramarital affairs. Mark begins to sense that Strong was conscious of the existence of a future biographer and sought both to hide things from him and to communicate indirectly with him. For example, when listening to a tape-recorded speech the old man made toward the end of his life, Mark realizes that a veiled reference to the secret love affair was probably intended to be understood only by his future biographer. The two-way relationship between the men is further demonstrated by the way Strong has in a sense reached a hand through time and meddled in Mark's life: he has provided him with occupation for a period of three or four years and has "introduced" him to his granddaughter, with whom Mark falls in love.

This phenomenon of a personal, almost mystical relationship between a living and a deceased person of two different eras is one that fascinates Lively, interested as she is in the plastic, mysterious nature of time. We will recall that she portrayed this same phenomenon in her children's book *The Ghost of Thomas Kempe,* in which 10-year-old James Harrison develops a "friendship" with Arnold Luckett, the little boy whose aunt owned the Harrisons' cottage in the mid-nineteenth century and whom James gets to "know" by reading old diaries and letters discovered in the attic. Just as Arnold indirectly advises James on how to banish the ghost that has been menacing the cottage for centuries, so Strong reaches a hand through time and manipulates Mark. And both Mark and James are prone to envisioning their "friend" as an amalgam of ages, for they possess an omniscient perspective on the deceased person's life (Mark of course knows how Strong's life turned out, and James learns that Arnold grew up to be an educator and founded the village school, where a portrait of him in middle age now hangs). Both protagonists, then, share with Lively and many of her other characters a sensitivity to "time warps."

James, with a child's freedom from the gridlock hold realism and rationality have on the mind, believes quite literally in such warps. Mark does, too, in certain moods, when it strikes him as "impossible that the historic past was extinguished, gone; surely it must simply be somewhere else, shunted into another plane of existence, still peopled and active and available if only one could reach it."[3] But for the most part, time warps in Lively's adult novels have more to do with the protagonist's sensitivity to echoes of the past than with actual emergences of earlier times. Thus, Mark's rapport with Strong essentially grows out of his imaginative and intellectual efforts to experience the world from the point of view of someone living in a bygone era.

In addition to perusing Strong's correspondence, Mark's research involves interviewing a number of people who had known the writer, and it is mainly in these scenes that Lively demonstrates her flair for satire and comedy of manners. For example, her portrait of Stella Bruce, Strong's aged former mistress, who adorns herself with jewelry and make-up and drops coy hints about past sexual alliances, calls to mind the lascivious dowagers of Restoration comedy. And in her sketch of Major Hammond, the octogenarian whose aunt was Strong's great love, Lively has captured perfectly the Dickensian eccentricities of the stereotypical rural bachelor, garbed in tattered tweeds, drinking whiskey at 10

A.M., and comfortably surrounded by his hunting trophies, dogs, and gumboots.

Two other comical portraits are of Strong's bikini-clad 62-year-old daughter, Hermione (Carrie's mother), and of her pretentious artist lover, 20 years her junior. Hermione is a coarser version of *Treasures of Time*'s Laura Paxton: both are stunningly egotistical, name-dropping women who seem totally insensitive to others, especially to their daughters, on whose psychological development their overbearing personalities have had disastrous effects. Just as Laura does in her public reminiscences about life with her late famous husband, Hermione paints an absurdly distorted, self-centered picture of her childhood with a famous father. And Hermione's shirtless, jeans-clad boyfriend, Sid, is a marvelously comic creation, a caricature of the type of artist who, in a kind of reverse snobbism, feigns working-class roots, speaking "with strident south London diction, a fractured language composed entirely of colloquialisms spattered with foreign words and rendered in phrases rather than sentences, like a character in a comic fettered by the requirements of balloon speech" (*AM,* 136). Sid is ludicrously oblivious to the irritation these affectations trigger in others, such as Mark, who forms a dislike of him "so violent that he had to avoid looking at him. Every time Sid spoke Mark's irritation became physical: his crotch itched and his head began to ache" (*AM,* 136).

The Love Affair Plot Strand

Less successful is the novel's other major plot strand, the account of Mark's falling in love with Strong's granddaughter, Carrie Summers. Because the cache of letters Mark discovers at Strong's former home is too cumbersome for him to transport back to London, he must spend several days a week at Dean Close over the course of the ensuing summer. In so doing, he becomes increasingly attracted to and obsessed by Carrie, to the extent that he has difficulty concentrating on his work and is made miserable by her indifference. He goes so far as to work out a ploy to get her to spend a romantic holiday abroad with him: he convinces her to accompany him on his interview visit to her mother, who lives in the south of France. En route Carrie, who is aware of Mark's infatuation, consents to sleep with him, hoping this will help banish his obsession, but it doesn't. What finally does resolve the situation is the arrival of Mark's wife, Diana, who joins them as planned at Hermione's a week later, immediately sniffs out the truth, and orders an end to the affair.

There are a number of ways in which this plot strand lacks credibility. First, as many reviewers have pointed out, it is highly unlikely that someone like Mark would fall for someone like Carrie. Shy, awkward, and, thanks to a haphazard upbringing by the feckless Hermione, barely educated, she is the polar opposite of the bookish, sophisticated woman Mark is normally attracted to, such as the clever Diana. The evolution of his passion is also unconvincing: we are *told* he feels passion but we are not *shown* it; it is not conveyed in the same kind of visceral way as is, for example, his irritation with Sid or his intellectual absorption in his research. Indeed, he seems to take a very clinical, detached approach to the whole phenomenon, analyzing and discussing it with Carrie as if it were some sort of illness (she tells him that she hopes "it might be sort of getting better" and he replies that the "condition tends to be a bit more enduring than that" [*AM*, 86]). And when the two of them eventually go to bed together, there is a matter-of-fact quality to the experience that belies Mark's claim to be madly in love with her and that seems out of character for the naive, childlike Carrie.

Finally, the confrontation scene between Diana and Carrie does not ring true to real life. Diana supposedly loves her husband, and their marriage has been monogamous for going on 20 years; one would therefore expect her to be devastated—or at least hurt and jealous—when she discovers his infidelity. Instead, she reacts in a brisk, practical manner, immediately taking the situation in hand and trying to straighten it out, more like a mother resolving a fracas among her naughty children than a wife who has been wronged by the husband she loves. This episode is an instance of Lively's sacrificing verisimilitude for comedy of manners, for the scene is as humorous as it is unlikely, with Diana continually getting sidetracked by incidental and peripheral aspects of Carrie's confession. For example, when Carrie, trying to be helpful, offers her opinion that Mark was beginning to get annoyed with her because she had taken to reading at dinner, Diana finds herself temporarily diverted by this comment: "Reading?" she says. "Reading what?" And then she catches herself and returns to the main track: "Oh, never mind. . . . Are you in love with Mark?" (*AM*, 144). The episode ends absurdly, with Diana ruminating aloud about ways she might redo the decor at Dean Close when she spends lengthy stretches of time there in the future, as she will now have to do to make sure Mark stays out of mischief. The whole scene has a kind of flippant Oscar Wilde quality to it, with manners rather than morals and emotions the central focus.

This plot strand is thus entertaining and humorous, but also passionless, unconvincing, and a bit hackneyed. The tale of a sophisticated older man falling for an untutored naive has been told over and over again, from Shaw's *Pygmalion* down to the popular film *Educating Rita*. The reader has the impression that Lively latched onto it as a handy device for exploring one of the novel's major themes, the contrast between a natural, spontaneous approach to life and a book-conditioned one. Although Lively always constructs her novels around particular ideas, she usually integrates them more organically into the plot. But because the credibility of the love plot in *According to Mark* is weak, the work's thematic scaffolding is somewhat obtrusive.

The Plot Strands' Conclusions

The research plot strand culminates in Mark's making a major breakthrough in the mystery surrounding Strong's personal life during the period 1912–14. A hunch he has about a secret romance leads him to Major Hammond and thence to another cache of letters, this one housed in the Major's attic and consisting of the passionate love letters Strong had written to the Major's aunt, then in her 20s and married but planning to leave her husband for Strong—a plan that was never realized because the young woman suddenly fell ill and died. This discovery radically alters Mark's understanding of Strong's character and causes him to rethink the approach he will take in his biography. We never see the form this biography does take, for the novel ends before Mark begins to write it. But we do see the approach he takes in a radio program on Strong he has agreed to put together for the BBC's "Writers Recollected" series: he creates a pastiche out of the myriad, often conflicting taped testimonies of the people he has interviewed, believing that this is the best way to capture the complexity of Strong's character. The novel ends in similar fashion to *Treasures of Time:* Mark, listening to a taped run-through of the program, is flooded with insights about the elusiveness of the truth concerning a person's identity, much the way Tom Rider is when witnessing the multifaceted picture of Hugh Paxton that emerges from the BBC television documentary on him.

The other plot strand—the Carrie-Mark-Diana triangle—is resolved in a somewhat unrealistic fashion. Following Diana's no-nonsense dictum at Hermione's that the affair must stop, which Carrie is only too happy to comply with and Mark resignedly accepts, Carrie sets off for a solitary holiday in Paris, where she meets and falls for a young Englishman named Nick Temperley, and the Lammings embark on a meandering journey home, both of them regarding Mark as a kind of convalescent recuperating from a temporary ailment. Once everyone is back in England, Carrie and Mark's relationship dissolves into a polite, embarrassed friendship for the duration of the time Mark must spend at Dean Close. Both have clearly changed: Carrie, now in love for the first time in her life, has grown up, and Mark, over his "midlife crisis," realizes anew his love for his wife. It is thus a tidy if not entirely believable resolution.

Character, Values, and the Influence of Austen

Lively's controlled style, her wit and irony, and her flair for comedy of manners have caused many reviewers to compare her with Jane Austen. *According to Mark* particularly invites comparisons with Austen's conception of character development. Permeating this novel are the eighteenth-century values that informed her vision of what constitutes a healthy character: moderation, balance, and equal proportions of "art" and "nature." Although Lively's notion of character and identity is of course more complex and modern, she does share with Austen a certain hopefulness about the possibility of human growth and an essentially comic vision of life. And in the Carrie-Mark plot she chooses to indulge this affinity by employing the same paradigm for character development that Austen used. That is, she presents us with protagonists who each possess an excess of a particular character trait and need to learn to balance it with its opposite. Mark is too immersed in art (in the form of books) and Carrie too immersed in nature. In almost diagrammatic fashion, each moves during the course of the novel from his or her end of the character-trait spectrum toward the middle as a result of becoming involved with the other. The pattern is reminiscent of that in *Emma* and *Pride and Prejudice,* in both of which the heroine develops in the direction of greater restraint and the hero in the direction of greater spontaneity.

From the outset of the novel Lively establishes that Mark lives almost entirely in the world of books. He spends his life writing books, and books have conditioned his thinking and supplied his major frames of reference. At the novel's opening, for example, while driving through Dorset on his way to Dean Close for the first time, he notes the way his view of the landscape has been influenced by Hardy's descriptions. He and Diana refer to famous authors and fictional characters casually, often on a first-name basis (Diana has a habit of "discussing the motivation of, say, Dorothea or Anna Karenina or Catherine Earnshaw as though they were acquaintances faced with tiresome but soluble practical difficulties" [*AM*, 91], and when Mark first explained to her who Gilbert Strong was, she asked, "Did he know Vanessa and Roger and Duncan and Virginia and all that crew?" [*AM*, 5]). In fact, some of their most serious differences have been over books; once during an argument in a pub about Diana's indifference to Russian literature, Mark caused her to storm out by snapping, "If you want to go through life as a person who's never read *The Possessed* then that's your problem" (*AM*, 37).

Lively's implication is that Mark is too ensconced in the world of books, at too many removes from real life. She informs us that early on he decided to write not novels but "books about other books" (*AM*, 22) and other writers; she portrays him as holed up all day, Casaubon-like, in his dimly lit study or his carrel in the British Library; and she suggests that he is beginning to fossilize: "He was forty-one, and on occasions thought wistfully of the blithe unpredictability of youth. He had not been much surprised by life for some while now" (*AM*, 2). Clearly, it is time for him to step outside his study and experience life unfiltered through the medium of books.

Ripe for a change, then, Mark is highly susceptible when he meets Carrie, for her approach to life is the direct opposite of his. If he is several removes from raw life and nature, she is, quite literally, immersed in it, with smudges of dirt on her face and hands, the product of days spent digging in the earth, planting and growing things. Although at first Mark, who is "not much of a gardener" (*AM*, 6), is indifferent to Carrie's work and contemptuous of her ignorance of books, he gradually becomes entranced with her and her way of life. He has increasing difficulty sitting at his desk at Dean Close and keeps finding himself gazing through the window, longing to be out in the open air. He begins to help Carrie and her partner, Bill, with the running of the garden center, and in so doing develops an interest in plants and horticulture, replacing his accustomed literature-mediated approach to nature with direct involvement.

Of course it is not nature solely in the sense of plants and gardens in which Mark needs to become more involved but also nature in the more general sense of unmediated reality. Lively uses the former sense to function symbolically for the latter and shows that Mark is becoming closer to nature in both senses: at the same time that he is becoming more involved in gardening, he is also gradually correcting his character imbalance, beginning to live less through books and to respond more spontaneously to life. For example, he becomes excited about traveling abroad, after years of being reluctant to leave his study for any extended period and preferring to experience his adventures second-hand, through books. He reads Strong's love letters and becomes uncharacteristically queasy about snooping into someone's personal life, whereas before he had always glibly assumed that any means justified the end of writing a book. And in the midst of working on the BBC radio program, he responds to the sudden urge to phone Diana simply to tell her he loves her, a whim the former, work-absorbed Mark would never have experienced.

Just as Carrie lures Mark from the art/book end of the character-trait spectrum toward the nature end, so he lures her from her end toward his. When he first meets Strong's granddaughter, he finds her shockingly unlettered. She has read virtually nothing (not even her grandfather's books) except Mills and Boon romances and has never even heard of the well-known authors whose names are household words for Mark and Diana and their set. A poor reader as a result of the spotty education Hermione's bohemian, peripatetic life-style subjected her to, she turned early in life to nature for entertainment and fulfillment. She developed a fascination with plants and flowers that eventually led her to enroll in horticultural college. This aspect of Carrie's character is convincingly portrayed. Lively, an avid, knowledgeable gardener, vividly conveys the deep satisfaction and bliss Carrie feels pottering all day among her plants or poring over hillsides in search of a particular tendril or seed-pod. Indeed, Carrie's absorption in nature is as profound as Mark's in books.

But as contented as Carrie is with her life, she begins to suspect she is missing something when she gets to know Mark and senses the contribution books can make to one's existence. She therefore decides to take a novel along to read while they are driving through France. Mark selects one for her; significantly, it is *Emma*. Although Carrie begins reading in a desultory, tentative way, unfamiliar with the conventions of fiction, before long she is intensely absorbed, so absorbed that, ironically, she irritates Mark by wanting to read at dinner and in bed, when he, for once, would prefer experiencing "real life." For the first time Carrie understands the satisfaction of involving oneself in the alternative realities found in fiction; as does Diana, she begins to discuss characters as if they were people she knew. So involved does Carrie become in *Emma* that each time she loses a copy she searches obsessively for a bookstore where she can buy another, ultimately going through a total of three copies of the book.

By the end of the novel it becomes clear that Carrie's introduction to books has effected a necessary enlargement of her imagination and of her intellectual curiosity, two areas in which she had been sorely lacking. Visiting Paris after the termination of her affair with Mark, she for the first time finds herself taking an interest in culture and history, and voraciously devours books to help her expand her knowledge. Lively also implies that the experience of reading fiction, in particular the experience of participating vicariously in Emma's emotional maturation, has increased Carrie's own emotional potential. When she gets to know Nick, the young man she meets in Paris, she goes through the same kind of emotional breakthrough that Emma does when she realizes she is in love with Mr. Knightley, experiencing for the first time ranges of feeling she never knew she possessed. Thanks to Mark and to books, then, Carrie has gained the imaginative and emotional depth that had been missing in her character.

Lively thus has her two protagonists develop from one-sided, limited individuals to more balanced, rounded ones, with a healthy admixture of art and nature in their responses to reality. Although, as discussed earlier, this plot progression lacks a certain amount of credibility and is a bit too tidily diagrammatic, it does help achieve the comic, Austen-like vision Lively is striving for.

Perception, Imagination, and Books

But Lively has an additional purpose in constructing the Carrie-nature/Mark-books dichotomy. Besides using it to set in motion her Austen-like portrayal of character growth, she also uses it to explore the question of how perception and imagination are linked. This is an ongoing concern in her fiction, often taking the form of an exploration of how cultural assumptions and images inform our view of history and the past. As a postromantic, postmodernist thinker, she believes that people—adults, anyway—do not perceive the world passively but rather create meaning for it via their imaginations. And the imaginations of the kinds of people Lively knows and usually writes about are in good part shaped by their exposure to literature and culture.

Steeped as he is in books, Mark Lamming presents a particularly striking demonstration of the way this phenomenon works. He cannot look at a landscape and see it simply for the physical fact that it is but must impose preconceived images upon it, seeing not merely a field and a plough and a church but a "Constable" field and a "Paul Nash" plough and a "John Piper" church (*AM*, 96–97). He drives through Dorset and notes the way his response to it has been conditioned by Hardy: for him "this lush emotive landscape had two dimensions—what it was and what it suggested. It was peopled twice over, both by the mundane mat-ter-of-fact figures of the transistor-playing girl who filled the car with petrol for him or the pseudo-military landlord of the pub at which they stopped and those other presences, in many ways more powerful: Tess and Angel Clare and Bathsheba and Henchard and the rest of them" (*AM*, 84–85). And as he traverses London, he finds "himself reflecting—in quick succession—upon Roman Britain, Whistler, Daniel Defoe, Harrison Ainsworth, Virginia Woolf. . . . The city, indeed, seemed to exist not just on an obvious, physical and visual plane but in a secondary and more mysterious way as a card-index system to an inexhaustible set of topics which in turn spawned other topics. The river always made him think of the Romans, because of some oddly luminous book on Roman London, author and title long since forgotten but whose insights lay around still in the head" (*AM*, 58).

As these reflections reveal, Mark is cognizant that his perceptions are influenced by the books he's read. And intellectual that he is, he likes to ponder this phenomenon, putting to himself such questions as "did the pleasure derived from landscape come from what you saw or what was prompted by what you saw? Did children find the world beautiful before people told them it was, or only after? Was it ever possible to look at anything, after the age of about four, without what you knew interfering with what you saw?" (*AM*, 97). Lively herself is intrigued by this topic and explores it here by means of her portrayal of Carrie Summers, a character whose responses to the world are as unconditioned by litera-ture and aesthetics as Mark's are conditioned by them.

The vast difference between Mark's and Carrie's responses to the world is strikingly apparent in their early conversations. An example is an exchange the two have that is prompted by Mark's expressing his desire to pay a visit to Casterbridge while he is in Dorset. When Carrie looks perplexed, he realizes his mistake and says, "Dorchester, I mean. Dorchester is really Casterbridge, in Hardy's novel. The Mayor of, and all that." Carrie pauses to think a moment and then responds in a logi-cal tone, "Then it really isn't Casterbridge, if it's in a book, it's really Dorchester" (*AM*, 85). Although Mark's interchanging the names

Dorchester and Casterbridge is in one sense merely a slip of the tongue, caused by his current preoccupation with Hardy, in another sense it reveals the extent to which literature informs his outlook and creates reality for him. Carrie's response, on the other hand, reveals that for her, reality is the unmediated external world.

Despite Mark's initial exasperation with Carrie's literal-mindedness, as noted earlier he gradually begins to find it charming and to envy her ability to experience "natural responses, uncontaminated by the wisdoms of acquired knowledge" (*AM,* 53). His yearning to throw off the influence of books is temporary, however, the product of a midlife crisis. As we have seen, Lively implies that he needs merely to temper his dependence on books, not rid himself of it altogether. Not only is the latter not possible; it is not desirable. Lively believes firmly in the power of literature to enrich our perceptions of and responses to reality: "We are formed, quite literally, by what we have read. We can be changed by a seminal encounter with a book. Each of us has had such an experience— and we think of it as an experience, quite as powerful in its long-term effect as love or work or where we happen to live. It is the cumulation of many such experiences that joins us to a culture" ("Writer as Reader," 14). As charming as Carrie is in her primitive, innocent state, she is far more interesting after she has ingested *Emma* and begun to furnish her imagination with the images of fiction—images that, as the years go on, will no doubt "lurk still in the head, half forgotten but forever potent" ("Writer as Reader," 16).

Biography and the Subjective Nature of Evidence

As is implied by the title, with its allusion to the apostle Mark's Gospel version of the life of Jesus, this novel's major theme is the idea that any account of a person's life is always partial, for it is inevitably limited by the point of view of the witness. This theme grows out of Lively's ongoing interest in the subjective way people interpret evidence, which she usually expresses by means of her kaleidoscopic narrative technique. Here the main strategy she uses to explore her theme is the research plot: Mark, like his New Testament predecessor, is trying to write a definitive account of the life of his subject, but inevitably can create only a limited, subjective one.

The difficulty of piecing together an accurate picture of a person's life is caused in part by the problematic nature of the evidence left behind— the gaps and omissions in diaries and correspondence, the misleading impressions created by photographs. But it is also caused by the subjective nature of witnesses' testimonies. The more people Mark interviews—Strong's friends, enemies, colleagues, relatives, and former mistresses—the more elusive the truth about the man seems to be. Witnesses' views are influenced by a range of factors, including their personal or professional relationship with Strong, the situations they viewed him in, and even their own personalities and psychological needs. And many of these views conflict with or contradict others to the extent that Mark concludes that a person's "life is several different lives, according to who is doing the talking" (*AM*, 165). Strong, for example, "may or may not have faked a travel book, exercised bribery and/or intimidation, been a loving husband and father, a domestic tyrant and marital trickster" (*AM*, 147).

Frustrated by the growing number of what he refers to as "lies and silences" in the evidence accrued, Mark is not sure how he can compose a complete, truthful account of Strong's life. Ultimately he decides that the truest account would be one that acknowledges the idea that there is no final truth about anyone. And therefore for the BBC program on Strong, he decides to let the "lies and silences" speak for themselves, advising the producer to present the conflicting taped testimonies with as little editing as possible. Mark himself, serving as the segment's commentator, sums up the contradictory accounts of Strong's life with a statement that captures Lively's theme succinctly: "We all know, with reference to our own lives, the curious ways in which truth can be not so much distorted as multi-faceted. Give the kaleidoscope a shake and a different picture forms. Each of us sees through a glass darkly, impeded not just by the frailties of memory but by our own convictions. We see what we persuade ourselves that we have seen" (*AM*, 212).

According to Lively, this subjective seeing applies not only to first-hand witnesses but also to the biographer himself. That is, the biographer is not merely a neutral medium through which the evidence is channeled into an objective biography; rather, as with the historian, the biographer's own biases and assumptions affect his selection and interpretation of evidence. We never find out what Mark's biography is like when completed, since the novel ends before he commences writing it, but we know it will not be an objective account of Strong's life: it will be Strong's life "according to Mark." The book will no doubt be pervaded, for example, by the poststructuralist assumption, which Mark has absorbed from the times and the intellectual climate he lives in, that there is no such thing as absolute truth and that a person's identity is the intersection of other people's views of him. Mark's account will be further colored by his own emotional make-up: having gone through a midlife crisis that has caused him to appreciate more fully the life of the emotions, he will no doubt emphasize the important role played by Strong's secret love affair in his personal development. The biography, then, will reflect both the larger cultural assumptions of Mark's era and his own particular attitudes and biases.

The novel ends with an endorsement of the idea that all we know of other people are simply versions of themselves. Throughout the book Mark has applied his insights about biography to his own life, noting how he presents not his "true self" but versions of himself to others. Indeed, his own identity seems to be as elusive as Strong's: Mark has "become aware—uncomfortably aware—of the unreliability of one's own testimony; sometimes he listened to his own edited or amended accounts of things, as related to Diana or to friends. He remembered, as a small boy, being exhorted to tell the truth; at that point one had been given the impression that this was a perfectly simple matter—you did not say that things had happened which had not, neither did you say that things which had not happened had. What was not explained was the wealth of complexity surrounding this basic maxim" (*AM,* 21).

The elusiveness of the truth about self is demonstrated dramatically to Mark during the BBC studio session when he is taken aback by the sound of his own voice on the tape recorder: it is at first "unfamiliar—as though for an instant you did indeed hear what others hear" (*AM,* 210); the "smooth, pedantic" (*AM,* 212) tone projects a version of himself that he dislikes and currently feels alienated from. But Mark realizes that this is what the people who will listen to the radio program will take to be his true self. And so, when he leaves the studio at the end of the tape review session, he knows that he has left a version of himself there, recorded on the tape that the public and posterity—perhaps even a future biographer of Mark himself—will have as evidence of him. The novel's final words are fitting: "And so they part, the producer to his office somewhere and Mark into the street, leaving locked away there Hermione and the Major and the rest of them. And, now, himself" (*AM,* 218).

Conclusion

This novel is yet another demonstration of Lively's ability to combine elements of comedy of manners with those of the novel of ideas. It also points again to her affinity with the sensibilities of a range of literary periods. That is, at the same time that she asserts poststructuralist views about the tenuous nature of reality and of personal identity, she also explores such eighteenth-century concerns as the art versus nature conflict and the salubriousness of moderating one's character extremes. Thus, despite its occasional lapse into stereotype and cliché, *According to Mark* is a rich, complex novel.

Chapter Seven
Moon Tiger

Lively's seventh novel, *Moon Tiger* (1987), is the most impressive display to date of her unconventional narrative methods and her characteristic themes of history, memory, evidence, and the subjective nature of reality. Winning the prestigious Booker Prize (England's yearly award for best fiction), *Moon Tiger* thrust Lively into the literary limelight on both sides of the Atlantic and as far away as Australia and Singapore. The result has been an enormous increase in sales for all her books, an inundation of fan mail and speaking invitations, and contacts by movie producers interested in making a film version of *Moon Tiger*. Lively finds the attention flattering but time-consuming, and she now has to be more deliberate in setting aside periods of uninterrupted time for writing.

The idea for *Moon Tiger* had been gestating in the author's mind for many years. The experience of growing up in Egypt left her with a vivid sense of that country, but it was a child's sense, comprising images and impressions rather than facts and knowledge. Although the Desert War formed a backdrop to her childhood, she understood very little of what was going on at the time; nor did she know anything about the history of Egypt. It wasn't until Lively revisited this country for the first time, in 1984, and looked at it through the eyes of an adult and a trained historian that she hit upon a way to forge her childhood experience into a nonautobiographical novel. The result was *Moon Tiger*, which portrays the life of an English historian and journalist stationed as a war correspondent in North Africa during the Rommel campaign of 1942. Although only a part of the story is set in Egypt—the rest being set in Dorset, where Claudia, the protagonist, grows up, and London, where she lives as an adult—it is, as we shall see, the central part. To create this picture of wartime Egypt, Lively explains, she needed to draw on a "fusion of sources—war memoirs and diaries, the archive of still photographs and film kept at the Imperial War Museum in London, the observations made on my first return to Egypt as an adult, and, perhaps most important of all, the anarchic and uncomprehending vision of my own eight year old self—seeing the streets of Cairo teeming with troops and military traffic, hearing the language and talk of that time, but not understanding it. Until now" ("Fiction and Reality," 18–19). Indeed, Lively's experience in writing this book nicely illustrates the way memories retained from childhood are intricately woven into adult consciousness, one of the very themes the author is concerned with in her fiction.

Lively's evocation of wartime Egypt has received wide praise. With almost poetic description, she captures its atmosphere along with its sights, sounds, and smells: the "teeming polyglot" (*MT,* 88) streets of Cairo; the ubiquitous musty odor of camel dung and kerosene; the ethereal beauty of white felucca sails dotting the Nile; the winking heat of the desert; and the decadent nightclub scene, in which young soldiers on a few hours' leave try desperately to drown their terror in sybaritic excesses. Even more impressive is Lively's rendering of battlefield scenes. Although Claudia of course does not participate in combat, Lively gives us a glimpse of it through the conversation and the diary entries of Claudia's lover, a young British tank commander who is eventually killed in action. Lively was initially unsure about the effectiveness of this aspect of the novel, for she knew that "it's sticking one's neck out quite a long way for a middle-aged lady novelist to write from the point of view of a 32-year-old tank officer" (Smith, 48). She has therefore found the critics' ample praises of the battlefield segments reassuring. Most gratifying have been the letters from old veterans of the Western Desert Campaign who tell her the book "is accurate. That's how it was" (Smith, 48).

The Plot and the Protagonist

Although concerned with World War II, *Moon Tiger* is not a conventional war novel or historical novel. That is, the focus is not on World War II per se but on the way in which war and other historical events intersect with and affect private lives, in particular the life of the protagonist, Claudia Hampton. The novel has no plot in the usual sense, but instead consists of a series of memories and flashbacks that occur inside the mind of 76-year-old Claudia as she lies dying of cancer in a London hospital. These are presented not chronologically but associatively, simulating the way memory operates. The narrative thus jumps among different periods of Claudia's life—her childhood, adolescence, young womanhood, middle age, and old age—and intersperses these memories and flashbacks with occasional scenes in time present. We thus gradually piece together in jigsaw puzzle fashion the facts of her biography, which are as follows.

Claudia is born in 1910 into a genteel, upper-middle-class Dorset family. Her father having been killed in World War I and her mother being a quiet, retiring figure, it is her brother, Gordon, who figures most prominently in her childhood. The two siblings, only a year apart in age, are "birds of a feather" (*MT,* 3): energetic, adventurous, intellectually precocious children who prefer each other's company to anyone else's. As she does in many of her children's books and in some of her adult ones, Lively here portrays in a vivid, realistic way the strong bond some siblings develop in childhood—a remarkable accomplishment given that she herself was an only child. Claudia and Gordon's relationship becomes even more exclusive and elitist during their arrogant teen years, culminating in a near-incestuous phase—indeed, there are oblique suggestions of one or two wholly incestuous episodes—before subsiding into a more conventional sibling relationship in their 20s. For the rest of their lives, the bond between the two remains primary, through Gordon's marriage to colorless Sylvia and through Claudia's series of love affairs. Right down into old age, including the last time they see one another two days before Gordon dies, whenever brother and sister get together the rest of the world pales and becomes background to their spirited, sparring conversation.

As could have been predicted, both siblings forge brilliant, high-powered careers for themselves. Gordon becomes an internationally renowned economist, affiliated with both Oxford and Harvard, his advice constantly sought by governments across the globe. (As this description suggests, Gordon strongly recalls *Perfect Happiness*'s Steven Brooklyn, and Gordon's relationship with Claudia bears a marked resemblance to Steven's with his sister, Zoe, who is also, like Claudia, a gutsy, outspoken journalist and a woman who refuses to conform to the traditional female role.) Claudia graduates from Oxford and goes on to become a well-known author of popular history books—publishing, among others, works on Napoleon, Tito, and Cortez—and a journalist with a reputation for grittily honest articles and exposés. Always wanting to be at the cutting edge of history, she finagles a position as a war correspondent—a job generally not made available to women at that time—covering the Western Desert Campaign. It is during this time that she also experiences the most intensive period of her own personal history.

On a foray into the desert to witness the aftermath of the most recent battle, Claudia meets Tom Southern, the young British tank commander whom she will describe decades later on her deathbed as having constituted the "core," the "centre," of her existence (*MT,* 70). Although Claudia, beautiful and sexually liberated, has been involved with numerous men in her 31 years, Tom is the first—and will be the only—one she falls deeply in love with: in the heady first few days of their relationship, she feels "as though she were in a state of grace. Calm down, she tells herself. Just because this has never happened to you before. Because you have reached the ripe age of thirty-one without knowing this peculiar derangement" (*MT,* 106). The two spend every minute of Tom's infrequent leaves together over the next few months, and Lively's description of this affair is, like her description of wartime Egypt, one of the most accomplished aspects of the book. In beautifully understated, compressed prose, she evokes a love of surpassing intensity.[1] For example, driving with Tom through the desert in a jeep, Claudia "sits there half-asleep, seeing little, just his hand on the driving-wheel, a brown hand with a scatter of black hairs between wrist and knuckles; forty years on, she will still see that hand" (*MT,* 87). Contributing to the intensity of the relationship, of course, is the fragility of its future because of the war. The "Moon Tiger" of the title is a fitting image for their situation: it refers to the green coil mosquito repellent that slowly burns on the bedside table throughout one of their hungrily hoarded nights together, dropping away into lengths of gray ash, a reminder of the inexorable passage of time and the precariousness of their situation.

The dreaded happens: Tom is declared missing in action, and Claudia experiences terror so overwhelming that, despite her agnosticism, she is driven to pray desperately in a cathedral. When his death is confirmed, she succumbs to utter despair. As Lively does in *Perfect Happiness* with Frances, she here demonstrates her ability to sketch in a few deft strokes a picture of someone overwhelmed by profound grief. The following concise paragraph, for instance, evokes the horror of Claudia's existence in the days following Tom's death: "The nights are worst. The days pass, somehow, because there are certain actions to be performed. The nights though are not seven or eight hours long but twenty-four—they are days unto themselves, hot black days in which she lies naked on the sheet staring at the ceiling, hour after hour after hour" (*MT,* 128).

But miraculously mitigating this anguish is Claudia's dawning realization over the next few weeks that she is pregnant with Tom's child. During their last time together they had talked of marriage and Tom had expressed his desire to have a child, and so this discovery, which under ordinary circumstances would have been greeted with horror by the unmaternal, career-oriented Claudia, is welcomed with joy. She is therefore devastated when, in her second trimester, she suffers a miscarriage. Thus when Claudia returns to London after the war, she, too, like the returning soldiers, bears painful emotional scars. For the rest of her life she will carry deep within her her love for Tom, putting up a steely, invulnerable front to the world but subject privately to moments of unbearable grief.

Claudia's career continues to thrive after the war and to involve her personal life with public events and historical movements. For example, the research for her book on Tito introduces her to Jasper, a career diplomat for the Foreign Office and an expert on Yugoslavia, with whom she becomes involved in a relationship that will significantly affect the rest of her life. Never really in love with him, she is attracted to his sexual charm and his exotic background—his father was a gone-to-seed Russian aristocrat to whom Jasper's English-born mother was briefly married in her romantic early 20s. Although Claudia's fascination with Jasper eventually fades, the accident of their producing a child together, when Claudia is 38, creates an inevitable tie. For the next four decades their unconventional liaison continues; they never marry but live together intermittently.

The result of their union is Lisa, a colorless child more like her conventional grandmothers, who are mainly responsible for her upbringing, than like her flamboyant parents. Claudia is, as she herself acknowledges, not good at being a mother, and the demands of her career make it difficult to raise a child. She sees Lisa as much as she can, but the two are never close, and on her deathbed Claudia continues to be amazed that this middle-class, Jaeger-suit-wearing suburban wife and mother is actually her offspring.

Another instance of Claudia's personal life becoming entangled with historical events is her befriending of Laszlo, a young Hungarian studying art in London, whom she meets as a result of a newspaper article she writes denouncing the Soviet takeover of Hungary. Laszlo's father gets wind of the article and, inferring rightly that Claudia is a sympathetic liberal, telephones from Budapest begging her to look up his son and warn him against returning home. Claudia invites Laszlo to her flat, sees what sorry straits he is in, and extends the invitation to a few days' stay. This gradually turns into a long-term arrangement, with Claudia becoming something of a mentor and surrogate mother to Laszlo over the years. Even after he finally moves out and sets up house with his homosexual companion, he and Claudia remain extremely close. Indeed, he is one of the handful of key people in

Claudia's life, along with Lisa, Jasper, and Gordon's widow, Sylvia, who visit her on her deathbed.

Shortly before she dies, Claudia instructs Laszlo to go to her flat and fetch a packet she has tucked away in a bureau drawer. He does, and when she is left alone to open it, we learn that it contains the diary kept by Tom Southern in his own final days. Six years earlier she had finally been able to bring herself to speak of her experience in Egypt, and had published an article about it in a Sunday newspaper. By chance, Tom's sister read the piece and, concluding that the author must be the "C." her brother had cryptically referred to in the diary that was shipped home to his family shortly after the war, sent the diary to her along with a brief explanatory note. In her last hours, Claudia rereads the document (Lively reprints it in its entirety; it is here that her impeccable research into the technical aspects of the war is so masterfully displayed). Finishing it, she is flooded with epiphany-like insights about the presence of the past, the way it persists so long as it is housed in someone's consciousness. And then she dies. The room becomes suddenly empty, filled only with the creaking sounds of inanimate objects. This impression of a void where there had once been life underscores the very insight Claudia had just before death: that reality and history are given meaning only by the operations of human consciousness.

The stark emptiness of the closing scene also serves to emphasize, by contrast, the richness of Claudia's former presence. Indeed, although *Moon Tiger* contains other important concerns and themes, it can be read for its character interest alone. Claudia Hampton is one of fiction's memorable females, reminiscent of the glamorous but tough-talking women of the 1930s played in film by actresses Katherine Hepburn and Claudette Colbert. One cannot help but admire her guts and determination, and the discovery that beneath this tough exterior lurk secret passion and grief makes her all the more attractive. Although, as a few reviewers have pointed out, Claudia can be annoyingly brash, egocentric, and insensitive (one reviewer cannot forgive her her treatment of Sylvia and Lisa),[2] Lively still manages to make most readers care deeply for her, probably because we are exposed to her intimate thoughts and thus learn of her fears and vulnerabilities.[3] By the end of the novel, we have gained a richly textured impression of Claudia's personality and life. As the following section shows, this is in good part due to the unconventional narrative structure Lively employs.

Narrative Structure and Point of View

In *Moon Tiger* Lively carries her technical experimentation further than in any other novel, and the effect is dazzling. The complex narrative structure comprises a chorus of points of view and a jumble of time frames that fracture chronology. Framing the novel is the action of time present, the span of a week or so during which Claudia lies dying in her London hospital bed. Scenes from this frame open most chapters and are interspersed throughout the novel. They are put forth in present tense by an objective third-person narrator who generally just reports dialogue and actions without sliding back the window on characters' thoughts. After each such scene the narrative shifts into an intimate first-person segment from Claudia's point of view, and we observe the way occurrences in the time-present scenario trigger a chain of thoughts that lead to a memory from some particular period of her life. She muses awhile in past tense on this memory, and then the narrative shifts into a flashback consisting of a kaleidoscopic sequence of present-tense, third-person limited treatments of the episode recalled, from the respective individual vantage points of those who participated in it. After this flashback sequence the narrative then returns either to the third-person time-present frame or to Claudia's first-person thoughts and recollections.

The novel thus moves in and out of different time periods and back and forth among various points of view. It is a technique that in the hands of a lesser artist could result in confusion or redundancy or in an impression of experimentation for the sake of experimentation. But in Lively's skillful hands the effect is to create a mosaic picture of Claudia's life and to vivify the novel's themes, which center on the dominance of psychological time in the human consciousness and the elusiveness of any final truth about reality.

The Mosaic Quality of Claudia's Life

The multiple-points-of-view approach Lively uses in this novel effects a truer, more richly textured impression of the protagonist's life than would a conventional single-angle approach. By receiving not only Claudia's but also other characters' interpretations of the events in Claudia's life, we gain a fuller, more complex picture of this woman. We come to see that she is a composite of all the versions of herself that are presented in the book. These include the sharp-witted, iconoclastic intel-

lectual she perceives herself to be; the frail, confused old lady the medical staff see; the loud, stubborn woman many of her colleagues and
acquaintances judge her to be; the self-centered elitist her sister-in-law
Sylvia experiences; the generous, capable patroness Laszlo idolizes; the
cold, preoccupied mother Lisa shrinks from; and the passionate soul
mate Tom Southern loves. This technique also demonstrates the weblike
quality of Claudia's life: the way it intersects with and is shaped by other
lives. As Claudia acknowledges, "My story is tangled with the stories of
others—Mother, Gordon, Jasper, Lisa, and one other person above all;
their voices must be heard also" (*MT*, 5–6). As the novel proceeds, this
chorus of voices becomes increasingly complex, and the portrait of
Claudia fills out accordingly.

Also contributing to the mosaic impression of Claudia's life is Lively's
nonchronological method of presenting events. By witnessing the memories Claudia keeps returning to, we come to understand which life experiences have formed her and lodged in her consciousness. We thus gain a
more intimate understanding of her than we would with a straight linear approach. For example, the way she keeps circling back to her love
affair in wartime Egypt suggests how central this experience is to her
identity; and, indeed, Lively artfully structures the novel so that the
most sustained account of this core experience makes up the core of the
novel—almost exactly the middle third (pages 70–132 out of 208). This
nonchronological, recursive narrative method simulates the way one
really does experience one's life: not as a tidy sequence of events but as a
swirl of rich experiences that one mentally returns to and reexamines
again and again.

"a lifetime is not linear but instant"

Lively, as we know, is fascinated by the concept of time and in her fiction
frequently expresses the view that chronological time is a human, not
an absolute or natural, construction. One way she makes this point
is to show how children, who are not yet conditioned by conventional
ways of construing reality, experience time. For *Next to Nature, Art*'s
Jasper, for example, time is elastic and immediate, and for Claudia and
Gordon as children, "time was personal and semantic (tea-time, dinner-
time, last time, wasting time . . .)" (*MT*, 3). Another way she makes this
point about the artificiality of clock time is to give us cutaways to
characters' consciousnesses, thereby revealing that human beings' intu-
itive way of experiencing time is psychological and personal: potent

experiences seem immediate no matter how far back in clock time they occurred. As Claudia points out when she recalls childhood episodes with Gordon that are sharply etched in her mind, "A long time ago. And yesterday" (*MT,* 8) and "That time went; it is also forever there" (*MT,* 140).

Moon Tiger being the most interior of her novels, Lively offers in it the most massive demonstration of her theory that, as Claudia expresses it, "a lifetime is not linear but instant. That, inside the head, everything happens at once" (*MT,* 68). The jumbled chronology reflects the way Claudia mentally experiences the key moments of her life: not in the order they originally occurred, but in an associative, emotional order. She herself is, like her author, preoccupied with this phenomenon and uses images of nonlinearity to describe it. For example, the near-incestuous phase of her relationship with Gordon remains in her mind "a necklace of moments" (*MS,* 139); a day of transcendent happiness with Tom in Egypt "is refracted, and the next and the one after that, all of them broken up into a hundred juggled segments, each brilliant and self-contained so that the hours are no longer linear but assorted like bright sweets in a jar" (*MT,* 107–8); and she claims, "There is no chronology inside my head. . . . The pack of cards I carry around is forever shuffled and re-shuffled; there is no sequence, everything happens at once" (*MT,* 2).

What Lively means by everything happening at once inside the head is that the reality of our key experiences resides as much in the mental reliving of them as in their original, temporal occurrence. Indeed, such experiences acquire more significance and illumination with subsequent recollections. Lively's flashback method of presenting these experiences suggests both the way they stay lodged in the mind and the way they deepen over time. Casting the flashbacks in present tense creates an impression of the immediacy and vividness of the event recalled: when the narrative suddenly shifts from Claudia's past-tense recollection into a present-tense dramatic scenario, it is as if the episode really is happening again. Furthermore, presenting other versions of the event besides Claudia's own, in the kaleidoscopic sequence, creates an impression of Claudia's grasping new facets of the experience with each recollection. Although in these flashbacks Lively gives us the private thoughts of other characters that Claudia would not have been privy to at the time, the method as a whole simulates the way each reexperiencing of the event casts new light on it.

The Elusiveness of Truth

In addition to effecting a rich, mosaic impression of the protagonist's life and demonstrating the nonlinearity of mental time, *Moon Tiger*'s narrative method also dramatizes Lively's thesis that the truth about reality and other people is ultimately unknowable, for interpretation is always subjective and limited.

By continually unseating the narrative's center of authority, the shifts in point of view underscore the elusiveness of truth. For example, the accuracy of the portrait we get of Claudia in the objective third-person time-present segments is undermined every time the narrative shifts into the first person, causing us to be struck by the discrepancy between the feeble, confused old woman Claudia appears to be in her interactions with the medical staff and the lucid, clever person her interior voice implies. The latter portrait seems more "true," and we accordingly find ourselves assuming that Claudia's point of view is authoritative. But then we are jolted out of this assumption when the narrative shifts again, from first-person memory to kaleidoscopic flashback, and we witness the way other characters experienced the episode Claudia has just recalled: the discrepancies between their interpretations and Claudia's undermine her authority. This is particularly true of flashbacks involving characters who are very different from Claudia, such as Lisa and Sylvia. The cutaways to their consciousness reveal that these women are far more sensitive and aware than Claudia, who is dismissive and contemptuous of conventional people, realizes. From their angle of vision Claudia appears self-involved, rude, and even cruel. The inclusion of their perspectives is therefore an especially effective way of drawing attention to the limitations of Claudia's perspective.

The ultimate effect of the kaleidoscopic manner of presenting episodes is to create an impression of individuals sharing the same physical world and participating in many of the same external events but mentally experiencing this world and these events in very disparate ways. By continually shifting point of view, then, Lively undermines the convention of positing a narrative authority and thereby drawing our attention to the fact that there is no final truth about anyone or anything.

The History of the World According to Claudia

In *Moon Tiger* Lively has once again created a protagonist who shares her own sensibility of the presence of the past—Claudia believes we are all

"sleeping histories of the world" (*MT,* 65), conditioned by and embody-
ing all that has come before us—and who is critical of conventional attitudes toward history: the popular attitude that the past is quaint and the
academic attitude that the historian can write objectively about the
past.[4] On her deathbed Claudia announces to a startled attending nurse,
"I'm writing a history of the world" (*MT,* 1), and then proceeds to
launch into a series of mental speculations about the radically different
approach she will take in this work, bypassing the conventions of
chronology and omniscience.

These musings strike us at first as merely fanciful thinking on
Claudia's part. Not only do most of her ideas seem impossible to exe-
cute, but she, with little energy and time left, is clearly not in a position
to undertake such a project. Like the nurse who responds to Claudia's
announcement with a humoring "Well, my goodness. . . . That's quite a
thing to be doing, isn't it?" (*MT,* 1), we assume the old woman is delud-
ed. But as we move further into the novel, we begin to see that Claudia
actually is writing a history of the world, albeit unawares, right before
our eyes. That is, the book *Moon Tiger* is in effect the kind of history of
the world that Claudia envisions: it emphasizes the connection between
the historical and the personal; it subordinates all of history to the mind
reflecting upon it; and it presents historical events in a jumbled,
nonchronological fashion, thereby capturing both the chaos of history
and the associative way historical events are experienced by the human
consciousness.

Claudia's history is at one and the same time a history of the world
and her own personal biography ("A history of the world, yes. And in
the process, my own. The Life and Times of Claudia H." [*MT,* 1]). Her
deathbed ruminations, which compose this omnibus history, glide back
and forth between historical events and personal, biographical ones,
creating a cumulative impression of the way Claudia Hampton's life
has interacted with and been affected by history. We learn, for example, that World War I took Claudia's father and World War II her
lover, that Soviet expansionism into Yugoslavia gave her the father of
her child and the Hungarian Revolution her surrogate "son" and lifelong friend. This juxtaposing of the historical and the personal is the
method used throughout *Moon Tiger;* historical events are always fil-
tered through Claudia's mind and hence are presented in an associative, nonchronological manner, the way they reside inside her head.
Thus, for example, Claudia's reflecting on the prayer uttered by a
ninth-century monk at Lindisfarne begging God to spare his compatri-

ots the wrath of the invading Vikings leads her to recollect the prayer she made at Lindisfarne at age nine, when, annoyed with Gordon for having beat her in a race across that spit of land, she begged God to eliminate him. This in turn causes her to recall a subsequent visit she and Gordon made to Lindisfarne just before the war, when she found herself remembering the monastic prayer and noted that with the threat of the Third Reich, "it was as though the Vikings were here again, the blood-red sails on the horizon, the tread of men heavy with weapons. And the sea-birds called and the turf on the cliffs was sponge-springy under our feet and full of wild flowers, as no doubt it was in the ninth century" (MT, 17).

We are getting, then, not an objective, chronological account of history, but "the history of the world as selected by Claudia" (MT, 1). She is very aware of the subjectivity of her approach and frequently draws attention to it with such comments as "Egocentric Claudia is once again subordinating history to her own puny existence. Well—don't we all?" (MT, 29) and "My Victorians are not your Victorians. My seventeenth century is not yours. The voice of John Aubrey, of Darwin, of whoever you like, speaks in one tone to me, in another to you" (MT, 2).

This portrayal of all history as being subordinated to the consciousness of the individual contemplating it—in this case Claudia Hampton—is enhanced by Lively's technique of treating Claudia's life as a microcosm of the earth's. A rich pattern of metaphors and images creates parallels between the protagonist's own development and the geological and biological evolution of the planet. Claudia equates her "beginnings" with "the universal beginning" (MT, 3), because the universe did not exist for her until she registered it in her consciousness. In a style reminiscent » of the Biblical account of God's creation of the universe, she describes her own dawning awareness of the world: "In the beginning there was myself; my own body set the frontiers, physical and emotional, there was simply me and not-me. . . . And when I became a child there was Claudia, who was the centre of all things, and there was what pertained to Claudia, out at which I looked, the world of others, observed but not apprehended, a Berkeleyan landscape which existed only at my whim" (MT, 187).

Just as Claudia equates her own creation with the creation of the universe, so she likens her early childhood with the early eras of the earth's history. Her reflections on the rocks, ammonites, and crustaceans of the Paleolithic era are followed by recollections of scrambling among such rocks and fossils on Dorset beaches in her own "pre-historic" (early childhood) era. In very old age when she looks back at earlier stages of her life, they seem as long ago as the earth's earlier stages. For example, after a flashback to Lisa at age six, she thinks, "That Lisa . . . is as dead now as ammonites and belemnites, as the figures in Victorian photographs, as the Plymouth settlers" (*MT,* 46). And like the earth, she too has developed "strata" as she has aged; for her these are the experiences and relationships that have formed her identity and created the texture of her life. She frequently uses this term to describe Jasper, Lisa, Laszlo, her experience in Egypt, and so on. Finally, just as the earth contains a core beneath its strata, so does Claudia: her core is the love affair with Tom Southern, the most profound experience of her life.

Claudia's physical development, as well, is a microcosm of the planet's. Just as a geologist can learn about the earth's physical history by excavating, so could a pathologist learn about hers by performing an autopsy: "My body records certain events; an autopsy would show that I have had a child, broken some ribs, lost my appendix" (*MT,* 166). Furthermore, her body "remembers Java Man and Australopithecus and the first mammals and strange creatures that flapped and crawled and swam. Its ancestries account, perhaps, for my passion for climbing trees when I was ten and my predilection for floating in warm seas. It has memories I share but cannot apprehend. It links me to the earthworm, to the lobster, to dogs and horses and lemurs and gibbons and the chimpanzee" (*MT,* 166–67).

In summary, Lively's treatment of history in *Moon Tiger* suggests that human beings are "sleeping histories of the world" in two major senses: in that our bodies, language, attitudes, and customs contain vestiges of earlier cultures and forms of life, and in that "time and the universe lie around in our minds" (*MT,* 65), awakened into significance only when we think about them. In a sense, then, history comes into existence only when someone contemplates it. This point is dramatically underscored when Claudia dies and an eerie void suddenly replaces the rich human consciousness that had filled the room. The point is further underscored by the novel's closing sentence, "And beside the bed the radio gives the time signal and a voice starts to read the six o'clock news" (*MT,* 208), conjuring up an impression of a mechanical voice reciting world events to an empty, uncomprehending room, events that are meaningless apart from a human mind reflecting upon them.

Language and Reality

Another interest of Lively's that is explored in this novel is the relationship between language and reality. Claudia, like so many of Lively's
other protagonists, is an agnostic who has moments of existential anxiety when she reflects on the inherent meaninglessness and chaos of reality. As we have seen, to keep such feelings at bay Lively's characters latch
on to "tethers" that make them feel anchored to a solid world—familiar
people, objects, and routines, as well as conventional constructs for
mediating reality. Among these last, clock time and language particularly interest the author.

Although Lively's characters are very aware that chronological time is
merely a human, not an absolute, construct, they nevertheless rely on it
to give an illusion of order to the universe. Indeed, as we have seen with
Perfect Happiness's Frances Brooklyn, they are filled with panic when they
lose their grip on this kind of time. Language is another such anchor, a
way to impose shape, structure, and meaning on reality. As Claudia says,
"I control the world as long as I can name it" (*MT,* 51). For this reason,
she experiences a panic similar to Frances's when, owing to a combination of illness, medication, and old age, she temporarily forgets the name
of a familiar object in her hospital room, a curtain: "Today language
abandoned me. I could not find the word for a simple object—a commonplace familiar furnishing. For an instant, I stared into a void.
Language tethers us to the world; without it we spin like atoms. Later, I
made an inventory of the room—a naming of parts: bed, chair, table,
picture, vase, cupboard, window, curtain. Curtain. And I breathed
again" (*MT,* 41).

Claudia clings to language the way the religious cling to God, and
indeed there are religious overtones to her statement "I have put my
faith in language" (*MT,* 51), much as there are to Clare Paling's "I . . .
believe in language" (*JD,* 119). For Clare and Claudia and numerous
other agnostic characters in Lively's fiction, language possesses the
God-like power of investing reality with meaning, or, put another way,
of creating reality. Looked at this way, reality is just another text. This
belief is implied by Gordon's remarking to Claudia, when he knows his
death is imminent, "One resents being axed from the narrative" (*MT,*
184), and by both Tom's and Claudia's referring to their lives as "stories" ("The story continues; I am still in it" [*MT,* 204], writes Tom in his
diary, expecting any day to be blown up; and "We are no longer in the
same story" [*MT,* 206], thinks Claudia when she reads this diary 40

years later). Conversely, texts are in a sense as real as reality. Claudia observes that "truth is tied to words, to print, to the testimony of the page. Moments shower away; the days of our lives vanish utterly, more insubstantial than if they had been invented. Fiction can seem more enduring than reality. Pierre on the field of battle, the Bennet girls at their sewing, Tess on the threshing machine—all these are nailed down for ever, on the page and in a million heads" (*MT,* 6). And Tom, surrounded by the unreal reality of war, latches onto a tattered copy of *Dombey and Son* and, as he describes in his diary, "hunched in a bivouac in the shade of the tank, crawling with flies, [is] lost, transported, for hours on end, beyond all this, anaesthetised—ah, the miracle of words, of narrative" (*MT,* 204–5).

The miracle of words and of narrative is powerfully brought home to Claudia at the end of the novel when Tom's diary vividly revives him for her. "All I can think, when I hear your voice," she mentally addresses the dead man, "is that the past is true" (*MT,* 207). The idea that once dead, a person, like history, continues to exist only if housed in someone's mind has from time to time filled her with panic, just as it did Frances Brooklyn after Stephen died, but the existence of this diary means that Tom will survive after she is gone, brought to life whenever someone reads his words. And although Claudia herself is extinguished at the end of the novel, she too will continue to exist in the form of words—specifically, in the form of *Moon Tiger,* which embodies the consciousness and hence the reality of Claudia Hampton.

The Feminist Subtext

The feminist impulse we noted in some of Lively's earlier novels expresses itself most fully in *Moon Tiger.* Certainly Claudia is a model of the liberated woman: rejecting the restrictions of wifehood, motherhood, and traditional female occupations, she has succeeded in a man's world and expects to enjoy the same recognition and privileges that men do. But the feminist subtext in this novel is far more subtle and complex than the mere portrayal of a feminist role model.[5] Rather, it consists of an extensive subversive attack on established assumptions about reality, assumptions that radical feminists argue are male devised. Claudia rejects not only the traditional female role but also many of the values and belief systems that undergird patriarchal culture. For example, she expresses her disregard for society's ideal of the nuclear family by maintaining a loose, unconventional arrangement with her daughter (whom she has call her "Claudia" rather than "Mummy") and with the child's father. And she refuses to worship "God the Father." Indeed, she even in a sense usurps his place as creator and center of the universe, as is implied in her Genesis-like intonation, "In the beginning there was myself" (*MT,* 187), in her claim that she controls the world by naming it (*MT,* 51), and in her presentation of her own life as coterminous with the history of the world.

Claudia's skepticism regarding conventional ways of viewing and writing about history is in part a rejection of the male outlook, for these conventions have been established by men. The "dessicated don[s]" (*MT,* 14) of the academy are responsible for the widely accepted notion that history is an orderly chronology of public events and that these events can be illuminated by an objective, omniscient historian. Claudia, of course, flies in the face of these conventions, asserting, "Not for me the cool level tone of dispassionate narration" (*MT,* 8) and experimenting with different points of view and nonlinear order.

Claudia's iconoclastic approach to both history and biography implies an essentially feminist understanding of the relationship between self and world. Her rejection of the idea that the historian is a discrete intelligence separate from the world he or she describes, along with her belief that her story merges with other people's stories and that "unless I am a part of everything I am nothing" (*MT,* 207), supports the theory of feminist psychologists that women's ego boundaries are more fluid than males'. Nancy Chodorow believes that this is due in part to the fact that females do not have to separate their identities as completely from the mother following infancy as do males and in part to the fact that "women's biosexual experiences (menstruation, coitus, pregnancy, childbirth, lactation) all involve some challenge to the boundaries of her body ego ('me' / 'not-me' in relation to her blood or milk, to a man who penetrates her, to a child once part of her body)."[6] Lively's kaleidoscopic multiple-points-of-view method creates a weblike effect, an impression of Claudia's identity merging with others', and hence validates this uniquely female sense of self.

Yet another way *Moon Tiger* attacks patriarchal assumptions and conventions is through its narrative strategies. Its continual shifting of point of view amounts to an undermining of the very notion of authoritative interpretations of reality. Furthermore, its rejection of plot can be interpreted as a rejection of patriarchal authority, if one accepts Roland Barthes' theory that all narratives are based on the story of Oedipus, with the protagonist's movement from ignorance to knowledge being an expression of the Oedipal search for one's father and true origins.[7]

Finally, *Moon Tiger* refuses to allow the love interest to dominate. Although Claudia claims that Tom is her core, this element of the story does not drown out others, as it does in traditional narratives about women falling in love. By structuring the novel so that Tom is killed in both the middle of the narrative and the middle of Claudia's life, Lively is departing from the traditional romance pattern, which culminates in either the heroine's marriage or her tragic death as a result of the loss of love. Instead, Claudia goes on to live a rich, interesting life for the next 40 years. The love interest, then, is subordinated to an accumulation of other interests: Claudia's involvement in her career, her absorption in history, and her relationships with Jasper, Gordon, Lisa, and Laszlo. The book is thus structured to reveal that although her experience with Tom may be her emotional "core," her "strata" are very much a part of her identity also.

Rachel Blau DuPlessis uses the phrase "writing beyond the ending" to describe narrative strategies like the above, which delegitimate the traditional romance plot.[8] She discusses a number of twentieth-century women writers who employ such subversive tactics. Although she does not include Lively (*Moon Tiger* had not been published when DuPlessis wrote her book), this novel serves as a consummate example of the approach she describes. Thus, while Lively's primary concerns remain history, memory, and the subjectiveness of reality, these concerns take on feminist implications in her seventh novel, her richest and most complex to date.

Chapter Eight
Passing On and *City of the Mind*

Lively's most recent efforts, *Passing On* (1989) and *City of the Mind* (1991), are in many ways very different from one another, with the eighth novel harking back to her earlier fiction and the ninth seeming to be an extension of the complex narrative methods employed in her seventh. Taken together, *Passing On* and *City of the Mind* thus represent a culmination of two of the major strains we have seen in Lively's fiction: respectively, the Barbara Pym-like "village and vicars" strain and the experimental, postmodernist strain.

Passing On

Passing On is a much quieter, more conventional novel than its dazzling predecessor. With its quaint village setting, its chronological unfolding of events, and its restriction of point of view to two characters and an occasionally omniscient narrator, Lively's eighth novel lacks the expansive scope and daring technique of *Moon Tiger*. Aware of this, the author was somewhat apprehensive about the book's critical reception. "Following a writer's big success," she explains, "the critics usually have their knives out" (Interview). But her fears proved unfounded: the book met with wide praise in both England and the United States and was on the British best-seller list for several weeks, even climbing to spot number two for awhile.

Inevitably, some critics found this tale about the retiring life of a pair of unmarried, middle-aged siblings to be dull. But the majority pointed out that despite its surface uneventfulness, the novel harbors profound truths about the extraordinary emotions of ordinary people. Anita Brookner, for example, says that it "is Penelope Lively's quiet but distinctive gift" to make lives of unredeemed mediocrity "seem full of interest, and, more important, worth."[1] Many critics remark that what keeps the novel from becoming just another humdrum portrait of quaint English life is the authorial shrewdness, wit, and compassion pervading it. As Victoria Glendinning observes, Lively's "sympathetic intelligence defies dullness."[2] And as always, critics praise Lively's understated, economical style. "Her deceptively gentle sentences appear to arouse a low level of expectation," writes Brookner, "but the sentences themselves are expert" (Brookner, 33); Sarah Gold praises the way "Lively remarkably fuses the comic and the tragic in a graceful, fluid narrative"[3]; and Richard Bausch points out that "Penelope Lively is blessed with the gift of being able to render matters of great import with a breath, a barely audible sigh, a touch."[4]

The book was in fact welcomed by many Lively followers who found *Moon Tiger* too clamorous and polemical, its narrative pyrotechnics too distracting. *Passing On,* with its deft blend of comedy of manners and moving interior monologues and its precisely rendered portrayal of modern village life, is closer to Lively's earlier fiction. The author employs her kaleidoscopic technique to a degree, but she does not foreground her thesis on the subjective nature of reality the way she does in *Moon Tiger.* Similarly, although the protagonists occasionally call up powerful memories, for the most part they are engaged with clock time and the narrative moves forward chronologically.

The Plot

Like Lively's other novels, *Passing On* is concerned with the influence of the past on the present. Here this interest takes the form of an exploration of the way parents mold their children's lives and continue to do so even after they are gone. Inspired by Virginia Woolf's alleged statement, "Nothing is stronger than the position of the dead among the living,"[5] Lively created a tale in which a mean-spirited old woman manipulates her grown children's lives from beyond the grave. The woman is Dorothy Glover, who dies at age 80 just before the action of the novel opens. Throughout her long widowhood, she had dwelled in the drafty old family home, Greystones, in a fictional Cotswolds village called Long Sydenham, where she was known for her crankiness and misanthropy. Living with her for her last couple of decades were two of her children, Helen, now 52, and Edward, now 49. A third child, Louise, 42, who figures only peripherally in the plot, managed to escape the clutch of their overbearing mother by marrying and moving to London, where she still lives with her husband and two teenaged children.

In the days and weeks following Dorothy's death, Helen and Edward discover how fully their mother has dominated their lives. Rather than experiencing a sense of liberation now that she is gone, they feel oppressed by her ghostly presence. For example, soft-hearted, animal-loving Edward cringes in guilt whenever he feeds his dog table scraps—

a practice Dorothy strictly forbade; and Helen, testing the waters of
freedom by venturing off on an unaccustomed clothes-shopping excur-
sion, "hears" her mother criticizing her frivolousness and vanity: "You
can't wear that sort of thing. . . . It's too young for you. You're fifty-two.
And too short and too fat."[6] It becomes increasingly clear to the reader
that Dorothy's cold, scornful attitude toward her two elder children
thwarted their social and emotional development: Edward is a repressed
homosexual who has always been too guilty and ashamed to culminate
his yearnings and who has channeled his emotional needs into caring for
pets; Helen is an "old maid" acutely conscious of her lack of sexual fulfillment. Dorothy's hand in creating her elder daughter's fate becomes
shockingly apparent when Helen, cleaning out a cupboard of old cloth-
ing, discovers in the pocket of her mother's old jacket a purloined love
letter from Helen's beau of 20 years earlier. In a Hardyesque scene, the
daughter conjectures with growing dismay on the very different course
her life might have taken had she known of that letter, which contains
a plea for forgiveness after a quarrel and a request that she meet with the
young man to discuss their future. Having never received the document,
Helen had attributed his silence to a lack of interest and so had let
the relationship die. Thus did her mother rob her of her last chance for
marriage.

By the time the novel opens, Helen and Edward have become
entrenched in their celibate, reclusive way of life. They socialize little,
restricting their dealings with the outside world primarily to their jobs,
Edward's as a teacher at a girls' elementary school and Helen's as a
part-time librarian. Much of the novel consists of description of the
daily round of their lives, and Lively shows her usual precise attention
to detail in these presentations. As she does in most of her other novels, she modulates between reportage of externals and cutaways to the
intimate contents of the protagonists' minds, with the narrative composed mainly of alternating third-person limited sections presented
from Helen's and Edward's respective points of view (although there
are times when the reporting becomes omniscient). These glimpses
into the brother's and sister's thought processes are often poignant, for
they reveal the private battles each quietly wages with self-doubt and
a sense of failure. We witness Edward, for example, anguishing
through a long sleepless night over his foiled emotional development,
and we share with Helen a sharply deflationary moment when, having
suddenly become infatuated with a middle-aged widower, she confronts herself in the mirror and realizes the hopelessness of her situa-

tion: "She stood to one side and observed this pathetic self-deluding fifty-two-year-old in a state of romantic yearning and sexual excitation. . . . She agreed with her mother: riding for a fall, driving nails in her own coffin, only herself to blame. And there was nothing, absolutely nothing, to be done." (*PO,* 81).

The narrative is punctuated with such plunges into the characters' private consciousness. But this is not to say it is an entirely static novel; on the contrary, it contains two well-developed plot lines. One concerns Helen's belated erotic blossoming. This is triggered by the flirtatious but meaningless attentions of the solicitor handling the settling of her mother's estate, a silver-haired, silver-tongued widower named Giles Carnaby. He is clearly a cad and a lady's man, and it does not ring true that Helen, normally astute in her character judgments, would be oblivious to this, nor that someone with her depth would be attracted to such a shallow person. (This aspect of the novel is, in my opinion, the book's only failing; apparently Lively wants us to believe that Helen's sexual and emotional needs cloud her judgment in this area, but she does not bring this off altogether convincingly.) Nonetheless, for several weeks Helen rides a roller coaster of emotion, soaring to peaks of happiness when some gesture or statement of Giles's gives her hope, then plummeting to lows of disappointment and embarrassment when such hope proves unfounded. She ultimately regains her senses and her dignity, however, and takes the situation in hand: she confronts Giles with her feelings, and when he admits his lack of reciprocation, she makes a valiant effort to put him out of her mind and to forge ahead with her life.

The other plot line involves both Edward's private emotional conflict and an external, more public conflict. As Lively often does in her novels that are set in villages, she constructs a clash between the forces of redevelopment and financial exploitation and those of preservation and ecology. The Glovers' next door neighbor, a builder named Ron Paget, has for years been trying to persuade the family to sell him the Britches, the large wooded tract of land they own adjacent to their yard, so that he can build a housing estate on it. Dorothy Glover had resisted simply out of stubbornness, but her children resist on principle: Helen because she has the usual moral and aesthetic qualms Lively's protagonists possess concerning modernization and capitalism, Edward because he is a committed naturalist and ecologist and has turned the tract into a preserve for endangered plant and animal life. Ron is also constantly nagging the Glovers to update their home and trim their yard, and they finally reluctantly accept his offer to send his teenaged son over to cultivate their gone-to-seed garden.

The presence of young Gary, a golden Adonis-like lad, proves a torment for Edward, stirring his long-suppressed homosexual yearnings. Increasingly agitated by Gary's presence, he finally loses control and makes an advance on the boy, who rushes home in horror and tells his father. The latter, unscrupulous exploiter that he is, attempts to bribe the Glovers with this information: he will keep his mouth closed about what happened if they will sell him the land. Edward is paralyzed with self-revulsion at what he has done and becomes incapable of dealing with the situation, but Helen, in a scene demonstrating her fine moral fiber, informs the builder that she will not be a party to bribery. Overcome by guilt and fearing that the world will soon know of his deed, Edward attempts to commit suicide, but is rescued in time by his visiting nephew and taken to the hospital. The entire situation blows over when Ron, assured by Helen that her brother is deeply remorseful and will never again approach Gary, decides, uncharacteristically, to do the decent thing and leave the Glovers alone (except that the subsequent death by "accidental" poisoning of Edward's dog seems to bear the stamp of Ron's revenge). Edward gradually recovers from his suicidal depression, as does Helen from her humiliation in love, and the novel concludes, in Lively's typical open-ended fashion, with the protagonists ready to muddle on with their quiet lives.

Determinism and Darwinism

With its grim plot, *Passing On* is one of Lively's darkest novels, resembling most closely the fatalistic *Judgment Day*. Like that work, *Passing On* is filled with reminders of human beings' powerlessness over their destinies, with the emphasis here being on the role played by parentage and ancestry in the construction of one's fate. Helen and Edward, now in possession of the hindsight of middle age, are beginning to realize how their passive acquiescence to their mother's influence has determined the course of their lives. Although Helen asserted her independence for a few years following university graduation, she eventually found it easier to succumb to her mother's hectoring about the pointlessness of pursuing a career away from home when she could get a good job locally and save money by residing at Greystones. Now, at 52, she looks back at that critical period of her life and perceives "with crystal clarity, the slide from indecision to an inevitable self-perpetuating arrangement; she saw how what might have been an undistinguished but useful career, dignified by such a title, had turned into a series of jobs. At the time, fatal steps are seldom recognised as such" (*PO*, 25).

But the role played by family in shaping one's life is not restricted to behavioral influence; genes and biology also play a part. Helen and her siblings are uncomfortably aware that they have inherited certain physical and personality traits from Dorothy: Louise has her wiry hair, and Helen and Edward have her flat feet and her tendency to be frugal. And once when Helen is conversing with her punk, shaven-headed nephew Phil, she catches, incongruously, a glimpse of Dorothy in the "curve of the nostril, something about the set of the mouth" (*PO*, 190). This causes her to be struck by the power of "genes, hurtling through body after body, willy-nilly, set on a course of their own" (*PO*, 190), "simmering away in the body like invisible volcanoes, harbouring intelligence and irascibility and shape of nose and the tendency to particular diseases" (*PO*, 191).

Such reflections are scattered throughout the novel. Edward makes similar observations whenever he has dealings with the parents of his young pupils. It distresses him to know that some of the open-minded little girls he teaches will gradually and insidiously become like their class-conscious, philistine mothers. Conversing awkwardly with one such mother at the school's annual Sports Day, he glances down at her daughter and can suddenly "see quite clearly behind her shoulder, like the aura visible to spiritualists, the woman she would be in thirty years time. There is probably nothing to be done about people, he thought, nothing at all, nor ever has been: processed, from the cradle to the grave" (*PO*, 139).

Contributing to this emphasis on biological and social determinism in *Passing On* is a pervasive Darwinian motif. The Britches, the Glovers' tract of forest where nature-loving Edward spends several hours of each day, serves as a backdrop to the novel and as such is a constant reminder of the law of survival of the fittest. Despite Edward's persistent efforts to foster fragile plant and animal life there, he realizes he cannot halt the inexorable course of natural selection. The nettles and brambles he cuts back inevitably reassert themselves and imperil the growth of wood anemones, bluebells, and other delicate plants; the squirrels and magpies he shoos away steal back and disturb the habitat of the tits, goldfinches, and other timid birds and animals that seek protection in the Britches.

Edward is also acutely aware of nature's essential indifference to human beings, and, like Lively, is at times appalled by this fact. One gorgeous

spring day, for example, when feeling lonely and depressed, he seeks
solace in an idyllic natural setting, but "the place did nothing, nothing
at all. It simply went about its business. And its business, of course, . . .
was that of survival—survival and reproduction. As Edward looked
around he saw everything determinedly perpetuating itself—buds forming, leaves unfurling, seeds setting, the whole place off again on the
same mindless uncaring cycle, while Edward stood there in the midst of
it, quite alone" (PO, 73–74). Edward's sister Louise frequently reminds
both him and Helen that this impersonal biological urgency extends to
all of the natural world, including humans. As the mother of two difficult teenagers, she is obsessed with this subject, often expressing her
astonishment at the irrational, animal-like way one's body rages to pro-
create despite what one knows about the ensuing heartbreaks and
restrictions of freedom. As an agnostic, Edward cannot believe there is
any kind of intelligence behind all these drives and processes of nature.
Indeed, he almost loses his teaching job when word gets out that he lec-
tured on Darwinism in his science class and refuted, in response to a student's question, the validity of the theological argument for creationism.

Evidence that nature is in fact "red in tooth and claw" (Tennyson's
brutal image, in In Memoriam, for the Darwinist notion of survival of the
fittest) abounds in the novel. Just as Moon Tiger is dominated by geological imagery, so this novel is dominated by images of rapaciousness and
victimization. A plethora of victims make their appearance, from the
maimed birds Edward's dog, Tam, is always bringing home, to the mice
Helen traps unbeknownst to Edward (who disapproves of killing any
animal), and ultimately to the poisoned Tam himself. But this predatory
behavior is not limited to animals and to the physical. The novel also
presents examples of human and social rapaciousness. In particular, it
portrays the way the aggressive forces of technology, real estate development, and capitalism are threatening many traditional English values.
(Helen even uses the expression "red in tooth and claw" to describe modern village life [PO, 34].) The Glovers, with their liberal humanism and
their appreciation of nature, embody such values. This is apparent in
nearly every aspect of their life: in their refusal to succumb to Ron
Paget's blandishments to make money off the Britches, in their anticon-
sumerism, and in their close attention to nature (in this last respect they
resemble many of Lively's other sympathetic characters, in particular
Next to Nature, Art's Mary Chambers).

A number of scenes demonstrate the clash between Edward and
Helen's values and the commercial ones that are rapidly taking over.

One of the most telling of these scenes involves a visit the two pay to a posh investment firm in London. At the urging of Louise's businesswise husband, who is exasperated by his sister- and brother-in-law's naïveté in money matters, Edward and Helen agree to seek professional advice on how to make the best use of their small inheritance. In a marvelously satirical scene in which Lively displays her finesse at comedy of manners, the dowdy sister and brother come face to face with a couple of yuppie "masters of the universe." Lively even indulges in a bit of Tom Wolfe-like caricaturing, referring to the men elliptically as "pink tie" and "striped shirt," respectively. The two financial titans are at first bewildered by, then condescending toward, and ultimately dismissive of this pair of country mice, who appear to lack an appreciation of the supreme importance of developing one's "portfolio." Like Ron Paget, the men cannot understand why the Glovers do not want to sell the Britches: "Helen explained why it was impossible to [do so]. This took a couple of minutes, during which striped shirt and pink tie sat back, long legs crossed and polite smiles of amusement or possibly incredulity on their lips" (*PO*, 91–92).

Lively's sympathies in this scene clearly lie with the Glovers and their values. Edward's terse assessment of the brokers—"What terrible people" (*PO*, 93)—no doubt expresses her own sentiments. And her indictment of them becomes unmistakable when she implies their obliviousness to nature: walking away from their office building, Helen notices the breathtaking sight of a flock of terns swirling and dipping above the river, and it suddenly occurs to her "that striped shirt and pink tie, and Julia [the secretary] of the leather skirt, presumably passed them by five days a week without knowing that they did so" (*PO*, 94).

But although Lively presents Helen and Edward as morally superior, she also suggests that their values are not appreciated by the modern materialistic world and are therefore in danger of extinction. She underscores this idea by casting the clash between the Glovers and the investors in Darwinist terms. As Helen becomes increasingly conscious of the men's contempt for her kind, for example, she begins to feel like a threatened animal: "had she been a dog, all her hair would have been standing on end" (*PO*, 92). Then during Helen and Edward's restaurant lunch following the interview, the brother and sister make explicit analogies between themselves and an endangered species:

"They made me feel like . . . some species that had got into the wrong time slot. That ought to be extinct."

"Do you feel more comfortable now?"

"Marginally," said Edward, glancing round. "I could put up some sort of valiant struggle for survival."

"You'd have to adapt, not just survive." (*PO*, 95)

A bit later in the meal Edward makes the observation, "I suppose the difficulty about us is that so far as money and possessions are concerned we're at a more primitive stage than the rest. We're not interested in surplus. It's like being aborigines or North American Indians after the colonists have arrived. When everyone else is busy accumulating they get bothered about anyone who is quite happy with a modest sufficiency," to which Helen replies, "And look what happened to the aborigines and the Indians" (*PO*, 96).

Helen and Edward are thus shown to represent values and a way of life that are threatened by the bullying forces of the modern world. Edward in particular is depicted as a victim: like the fragile plants he futilely attempts to foster in the Britches, timid Edward is struggling to survive in a hostile environment, in his case a society that values only manly, aggressive men. And both he and his sister, as a homosexual bachelor and an old maid, respectively, are in a sense a "dying species"— they have neither of them produced any offspring. The title *Passing On* can therefore be taken to be an allusion to the threatened passing of the humanist, naturalist way of life Lively values as well as to the book's more obvious passing, the death of Edward and Helen's mother.

The Novel's Affirmative Vision

Despite the grimness of the plot and the bleakness of the protagonists' lives, however, *Passing On* is not, finally, a gloomy novel. As she does in *Judgment Day* and *Perfect Happiness,* works that also focus on the constraints and losses that characterize human existence, Lively here offers an ultimately affirmative vision. This affirmation derives in part from the comic impulse that makes itself felt in even her darkest novels, undercutting their potential for hopelessness by continually diverting the depressing into the amusing. For example, the otherwise dreary spectacle of a pair of unfulfilled middle-aged siblings living together in shabby circumstances is frequently turned into the stuff of comedy, as in the scenes when Helen attempts to hide from her animal rights–activist, environmentally conscious brother her nightly pillage on Greystone's mouse population and her habit of using dishwashing detergent whenever he is away from home. Even Helen's poignant last-ditch attempt at love is shown to have its amusing aspects: there is something comical about the way this middle-aged woman abandons her usual staid habit of mind and indulges in giddy, schoolgirlish anticipation whenever the object of her affection stirs up her hopes. The cumulative effect of these continual resurgences of Lively's comic impulse is an impression of the humor and amusement to be found in the human condition. As does Jane Austen, with whom she is often compared, Lively seems to be gently and affectionately laughing at her characters and their follies. And as in an Austen novel, this pervasive attitude effects a reassurance that all is basically right with the world.

But it is not just the author's attitude that creates this affirmative vision; Helen's also contributes. This protagonist possesses certain character strengths, shared by many of Lively's sympathetic characters, that keep her from succumbing to despondency or railing against her unlucky lot in life. These strengths include a no-nonsense approach to living, shrewdness and humor, and a sensitivity to and appreciation of the gratuitous oases of happiness that dot even the most ordinary of existences. Although Helen experiences moments when she comes close to despair—as when she realizes, too late, that she has allowed her mother to thwart her life, and when she must finally accept that romance with Giles Carnaby is largely a fabrication of her imagination—her pluckiness and wryness always come to her rescue and force her to exert herself. For example, in the midst of her depressing chain of speculation about how different her fate might have been had she received the love letter purloined by her mother, she suddenly takes herself in hand and, as if to say, "No more silly sentimentalism," observes that in all probability "she would not have lived happily ever after with Peter Datchett. No one lives happily ever after. Very likely there would have been a further coolness or misunderstanding and they would have parted" (*PO,* 110).

It is this same no-nonsense briskness that causes her finally to shake off her schoolgirl infatuation with Giles. She stares the truth (his lack of reciprocation) unflinchingly in the face, acknowledges that she has allowed herself to behave in a passive, self-destructive way for the past several months, and consequently embarks upon a vigorous, therapeutic course of action. Like Frances Brooklyn recuperating from a similarly vulnerable emotional state, Helen hurls herself into a number of household tasks, with the express purpose of banishing her lethargy and depression. Helen's chucking out the unused contents of Greystones' cupboards and repainting much of the house's interior constitute the same symbolic gesture as Frances's disposing of Steven's old papers and moving to a new house: both women are unshackling themselves from the crippling hold certain aspects of the past have had on them and are asserting a faith in the future.

Edward, too, seems to have experienced a kind of catharsis as a result of living through emotional trauma. Like Helen, he has attained a new strength and self-knowledge by the end of the novel. His sister notices that there is "an alertness about him; he [has] lost the frozen passivity of recent weeks" (*PO,* 209), and she notes too a sign of her own recovery: her mother's "voice" has been finally stilled. Although the Glovers' external fortunes have changed little by the end of the book and they are still social misfits, the novel concludes on a hopeful, affirmative note. In the final episode, brother and sister experience one of those epiphany-like moments found in certain other Lively novels, in which the ordinary is suddenly illuminated with a kind of transcendent significance and beauty: on an afternoon in late October they gather in the sitting room at Greystones and, each suddenly flooded with an almost mystical peace at the sight of the brilliantly colored natural world beyond the windows, sense the beginning of a new interest in and commitment to life. The novel's final sentence is "Both sniffed the air; each, gingerly, made resolutions" (*PO,* 210).

Thus, although Lively fully recognizes the dark aspects of existence—its brutality, its riskiness, its randomness—she neither despairs nor rails. Indeed, as Anita Brookner observes, "The absence of anger [in *Passing On*] is almost palpable" (Brookner, 33). Lively seems to suggest that despite our lack of control over our destinies, we can cultivate habits of mind that make life bearable, nay more than bearable: interesting and, at times, ineffably beautiful. Helen, like Frances Brooklyn, Zoe Brooklyn, Clare Paling, and numerous other Lively characters, possesses such habits, which include an ability to appreciate the humor in human situations, a tendency to hurl oneself into practical efforts as an antidote to existential despair, and a propensity for experiencing ephiphanic moments of happiness, in which the natural world suddenly fuses with and is irradiated by one's emotional state.

The Place of *Passing On* in Lively's Oeuvre

Although *Passing On* is in many respects closer to Lively's earlier, more contained novels than it is to *Moon Tiger,* it in no way constitutes a step backward for her. On the contrary, the eighth novel seems to mark a new maturity in Lively's fiction. She explores many of the same themes—the difficulty of seeing the past clearly, the importance of striking a healthy balance between the past and the present—and expresses the same liberal, naturalist values that she does in earlier works, but her treatment of them is more subtle here. Whereas in most of her earlier novels she relies heavily on the statements and thoughts of characters to convey her ideas, here she curbs this impulse, instead allowing the themes to emerge from imagery and situation. Although all Lively's novels demonstrate her stylistic deftness and precision, *Passing On* does so especially; it is her most controlled and understated work of fiction to date.

City of the Mind

City of the Mind is at the opposite end of the spectrum from *Passing On*. It is almost as if, after a necessary quiet interlude, Lively recouped and reasserted the titanic energies and ambitions that manifested themselves in *Moon Tiger*. Like that novel, *City of the Mind* embraces an expansive scope: the entire city of London, past and present. It also rivals *Moon Tiger* in technical experimentation, continually interrupting the main narrative with an intricate series of subnarratives concerning events in London's history. Although the same readers who are uncomfortable with *Moon Tiger*—those attracted solely to the Barbara Pym/Jane Austen aspects of Lively's fiction—may resist this novel as well, most of Lively's followers will find it one of her most impressive works to date. She ponders weighty issues in the book—the nature of reality, the dialectic between subjective and objective—but never at the expense of its novelistic qualities. Indeed, as with all of her novels, one can read *City of the Mind* for its character and situation interest alone. It presents an intelligent, sympathetic protagonist grappling with familiar contemporary concerns and problems, and it includes a number of deftly rendered comedy-of-manners scenes. *City of the Mind* has received the same kind of critical acclaim as did *Moon Tiger*, with reviewers commenting on its complexity and its technical virtuosity.

The Plot

The novel takes place over an approximately six-month period in the late 1980s, and its protagonist is Matthew Halland, a 40ish London architect who, at novel's outset, has just come through a divorce and is consequently in a somewhat disillusioned, depressed state of mind. As she does in *Treasures of Time* and *According to Mark*, Lively here again proves that she can create believable, sympathetic male characters. Matthew possesses many of the qualities we find in Lively's other protagonists, both male and female: he is intelligent, wry, and astute, with the usual Livelyesque acuity concerning the historical associations of place, and he is also capable of strong emotion and sentiment. As is true of all Lively's novels, one of the major pleasures of reading this book is simply the experience of bearing witness to the thought processes of an interesting, analytical mind.

Much of the narrative is concerned with Matthew's reflections and responses as he goes about his daily work as a senior partner in a successful architectural firm. As we have seen in her treatment of Mark Lamming and several other characters, Lively is skilled at conveying a sense of the intellectual absorption one can feel in one's work. Her description of Matthew's "fascination with the variety and manipulation of landscape"[7] and of the "frissons of satisfaction" he feels "at a technical problem overcome" (*CM*, 132) rings true to readers who have experienced this kind of professional engagement. Matthew's attraction to architecture springs not only from particular aesthetic and intellectual leanings but also from a historical sensibility akin to his author's. Like Lively, he is an ardent believer in the importance of preserving the historical associations of old buildings and neighborhoods, but in an authentic, not picturesque, fashion. He is therefore contemptuous of architects and builders who turn out "old houses as pastiche reproductions of the past" (*CM*, 54), and he cynically remarks of those who attempt to create an eighteenth-century ambiance in their homes by putting up gaslights and paneling, "If they're after authenticity I hope they're also denying themselves such anachronisms as modern medical facilities and the various public services" (*CM*, 158).

A complex person, Matthew sometimes finds himself experiencing a conflict between his historical purism and his desire to take on challenging architectural projects. It was the strength of the latter that caused him to agree to design a highrise for the Docklands, the old wharves district next to the Thames that is undergoing massive conversion to a high-tech business and financial area. During the course of the novel this project is nearing completion, and Matthew is torn between his pride in the towering steel and glass edifice he has created and his qualms about participating in this wholesale ripping up of the past and altering of an area's character.[8] Mark's ambitiousness, however, never encompasses lucre. Like most Lively protagonists, he is a nonmaterialistic, moral person who is baffled by the worship of mammon. One of the novel's subplots involves the efforts of a wealthy, unscrupulous developer to lure and bully Matthew into assisting him with the redevelopment of a Spitalfields neighborhood. Matthew is appalled by the immoral tactics this thug uses to get working-class tenants to agree to vacate targeted buildings, and he steadfastly refuses to do business with the man. In both his historical sensibility and his liberal humanist outlook, then, the protagonist bears a strong resemblance to his author.

Equal focus is given in the novel to the protagonist's personal life. Matthew is preoccupied with the dissolution of his marriage, frequently pondering the reasons for the dearth of feeling between him and his former wife, Susan. His pain and confusion are conveyed by means of precise, telling detail: he finds it unbearable in certain moods to glance at the Victorian rocking chair he and Susan purchased together in the early days of their marriage, and he experiences the unsettling phenomenon of seeing superimposed on "the cool and distant Susan with whom he exchanges brief and necessary words" (*CM,* 39) "that smiling, intimate shadow-Susan" (*CM,* 40) of former days.

Particularly distressing to Matthew is his altered relationship with his eight-year-old daughter, Jane, now in Susan's custody. Lively has captured the special poignancy of the situation of the divorced father, forced to feed his emotional cravings on the thin meal of biweekly visits with his child. A great deal of the book is taken up with description of the weekends the two spend together, and the conversations between father and daughter constitute one of the most accomplished aspects of the book. Although Lively claims she is no longer as familiar with children's minds as she once was, her own children now being grown up, her portrayal of little Jane belies this assertion. From the tacky but cherished pink plastic hair clip the little girl insists on wearing, to the way she sniffs out in a crowd other children her age and "pays professional attention to [them], in the way that animals are most sensitive to their own species" (*CM,* 87), to the baffling metaphysical questions she unexpectedly confronts her father with, she is a thoroughly true-to-life eight-year-old child. Indeed, Lively's portrayals of children and of parent-child interactions are among the best in contemporary fiction.

Matthew's personal life also includes, in the first half of the novel, a relationship with a woman named Alice Cook, with whom he occasionally goes to bed. Their lovemaking is a friendly, physically satisfying, but somewhat mechanical act, with both partners accepting the limitations of the arrangement. For his part, Matthew has become disillusioned about the possibility of ever again experiencing anything more. His attitude changes when he becomes involved with Sarah Bridges, a young woman he first meets in a queue at a sandwich shop and later hunts down and begins dating; he finds himself, miraculously, falling in love again. Lively presents the evolution of their love affair in the elliptical manner she characteristically uses to portray this phenomenon, with the partners' growing passion and attachment suggested in understated but potent scenes and conversations. The relationship effects a kind of spiritual rebirth for Matthew toward the end of the novel, and the book concludes on the same hopeful but open-ended note as do *Passing On, Perfect Happiness,* and many of Lively's other works: Matthew is unsure about his future with Sarah, and he is still beset with various professional and personal problems, but he feels a new excitement about and interest in life—in his own words, a sense of "exquisite anticipation" (*CM,* 219).

Narrative Technique and the Foregrounding of the City

As the above account suggests, there is not a great deal of plot in *City of the Mind.* It is character rather than action that engrosses our attention, and via a combination of omniscient reportage and intimate third-person-limited presentations of Matthew's thoughts and memories, Lively provides us with an in-depth portrait of the protagonist. But her purpose here goes beyond character study: the novel's ultimate focus is not on Matthew Halland but on the context in which he is embedded—the city of London. By means of narrative perspective, style, and structure, Lively foregrounds the city. Much as Virginia Woolf does with this same city in *Mrs. Dalloway,* James Joyce does with Dublin in *Ulysses,* and Carl Sandburg does with Chicago in the poem of that title, Lively portrays London as a pulsating, palpable entity, fueled by the energies of the myriad lives that have been lived within it. She continually uses metaphors and personification to create this impression, for example, describing the city as "throb[bing]" and "pulsing" (*CM,* 66) and referring to "the weight of the place" (*CM,* 67). And like Woolf's London, which sweeps Clarissa Dalloway up in its "waves of . . . divine vitality,"[9] Lively's sweeps Matthew up in its "current" (*CM,* 1), its "torrent" (*CM,* 114), and its "streaming allusive purpose" (*CM,* 87).

Another way Lively suggests the palpable quality of the city is to continually list the stimuli that bombard Matthew's senses as he traverses its streets. Like Joyce's Leopold Bloom, Matthew Halland is a peripatetic protagonist whose job involves much crisscrossing of the city, and as Joyce too does, Lively highlights the sights, sounds, and smells the protagonist ingests in these peregrinations. For example, driving along Euston Road one morning, Matthew registers "a cacophony of sound that runs the whole gamut from Yiddish to Urdu, a global testimony reaching from Moscow to Sydney by way of Greece and Turkey and remote nameless birthplaces in Ireland or India or the Caribbean"; a pastiche of architecture from London's various eras, including "Victorian stucco, twentieth-century concrete, a snatch of Georgian brick"; and a medley of cooking odors from such ethnic restaurants as "Pizza Ciao, King's Cross Kebab, New Raj Mahal Tandoori, Nepalese Brasserie" (*CM*, 3).

Matthew's traversing of London effects an impression not only of the city's variegated, richly textured character but also of its weblike nature, that is, of the way its inhabitants' individual lives are inextricably and imperceptibly interconnected. Lively asserts this idea by frequently sliding, in almost cinematic fashion, from a close-up view of Matthew's activities to an aerial perspective, from which we can observe "the city's mysterious intestinal life" (*CM*, 76) and detect the mazelike pattern Matthew creates as his path intersects with the paths of other people. Some of these conjunctions are more obviously fateful than others; his fortuitous crossing of paths with Sarah Bridges, for example, promises to dramatically alter his immediate, and possibly long-term, future. But in even the most minor of conjunctions, Lively suggests, one leaves behind something of oneself and takes away something of the person and place encountered. Matthew's life is thus in a sense spread out all over London, and in certain epiphanic moments he apprehends this, suddenly glimpsing "his scattered hours—irretrievable, enshrined" (*CM*, 218) as he walks the streets of Covent Garden or Lincoln's Inn Fields or Cobbham Square.

Lively's point, then, is that a city is a composite, or a web, of all the lives inside it. The most radical technique she uses to vivify this theory is to intersperse the narrative proper—the tale of Matthew Halland and his professional and personal activities—with narratives of London dwellers of past eras. Although time shifts are a common occurrence in Lively's adult fiction, they are usually restricted to characters' flashbacks. But in *City of the Mind* she presents these episodes apart from any mind recollecting them (except, of course, the mind of the omniscient narrator). The ultimate effect of this technique is a dramatic demonstration of the palimpsest quality of place.

The novel's structure is composed of a continual shifting back and forth between the main narrative about Matthew and the subnarratives about earlier inhabitants. There are four of these recurring subnarratives: one concerning Jim Prothero, a volunteer neighborhood warden during the World War II blitz whose territory was several blocks in the old City of London; another concerning a Victorian child named Rose, a Dickensian-like waif who roamed the alleys around Covent Garden searching for food; another concerning the nineteenth-century paleontologist Richard Owen, whose home was located in what is now the Royal College of Surgeons in Lincoln's Inn Fields; and another concerning Martin Frobisher, the Elizabethan navigator who set sail from the Thames in search of the Northwest Passage.

Lively engineers these shifts with deftness and artistry, using a series of hinges, or linking motifs, to connect the main narrative to the subnarratives. The hinge is usually an emotion or insight Matthew experiences that is similar to one experienced by an earlier denizen of the neighborhood in which he finds himself. Lively's method is to cut at this point from the main narrative to the counterpart moment in the subnarrative and to play the latter scene out, in lengths varying from one paragraph to a whole chapter, before returning to the interrupted main narrative. Thus, for example, just after Matthew, strolling through Covent Garden, is seized by an inexplicable, almost mystical urge to purchase a posy of violets, the narrative cuts to little Rose, who sniffs out the hopeful fragrance of violets among the more pervasive smell of garbage and sewage; again, as Matthew gazes at the Thames from his Docklands building, musing on the way the river reaches out to the sea and to the globe beyond, the narrative jumps back 400 years to Martin Frobisher, standing in the same spot and absorbed in similar reflections about the beckoning unknown worlds to which the river leads; and Matthew's terror when Jane is almost struck by a car is the hinge into an account of Jim Prothero's loss of his own little girl, who perished in a bomb explosion in the same neighborhood where Jane's near fatality occurs. Again and again in this manner, Lively weaves a connection between Matthew's existence and the existences of earlier residents of the places he occupies, creating the impression of an intricate web binding together all of London's dwellers, past and present.

The narrative technique thus suggests that the energies and emotions people expended in a particular place are in a sense embedded there and continue to reverberate down through the ages. And so, just as the moments of Matthew's life are forever enshrined in the spots in which they occur, so too are the moments of all lives lived within this city. In suggesting this, Lively once again reveals a kinship with Virginia Woolf, who also at times seems to apprehend an almost mystical sympathy between human beings and the physical world that envelops them.

Indeed, the reflections of Clarissa Dalloway on this subject could well serve as an epigraph for *City of the Mind:*

> did it matter that she must inevitably cease completely; all this must go on without her; did she resent it; or did it not become consoling to believe that death ended absolutely? but that somehow in the streets of London, on the ebb and flow of things, here, there, she survived, Peter survived, lived in each other, she being part, she was positive, of the trees at home; of the house there, ugly, rambling all to bits and pieces as it was; part of people she had never met; being laid out like a mist between the people she knew best, who lifted her on their branches as she had seen the trees lift the mist, but it spread ever so far, her life, herself. (Woolf, 12)

City of the Mind

The title implies, and the author herself has claimed, that the main thesis of this novel is that the past of the city of London exists only in the mind of the beholder.[10] This theme, of course, grows out of Lively's ongoing interest in the subjective aspects of history and of time. But whereas in her earlier works she creates a picture of an almost solipsistic reality by emphasizing the discrepancies between different characters' versions of the same event, here she opens a window onto an objective reality by employing predominantly omniscient narration and presenting historical episodes that are not housed within a character's consciousness. At the same time, she continues to stress that history and reality gain their meaning only by the operations of human consciousness. Thus, a kind of paradox, or double focus, emerges in the novel: Lively presents the individual as embedded in a universe much larger than him- or herself but at the same time as housing that universe within his or her own mind, or, as she says of Matthew Halland, as being "a person of no great significance, and yet omniscient" (*CM,* 2), and of Martin Frobisher, as being "a pinpoint in infinity, and a universe" (*CM,* 122).

The pulsating, palpable impression Lively creates of the city of London, along with the omniscient presentations of scenes from its past, serves to assert that reality does exist outside the human mind. Indeed, the narrator continually stresses the point that the city itself is more enduring than the puny human existences it houses. But this external reality has no inherent meaning apart from what the human consciousness bestows upon it. Matthew expresses this idea in reference to a particular building: "This is a pile of bricks. Carefully arranged bricks, I grant you, but a pile of bricks none the less. You may call it a late

Georgian house with a neo-classical portico and Coade stone dressings. Others might just call it a house. A Martian would call it a pile of bricks, if he had got as far as identifying a pile or a brick" (*CM,* 26). Raw reality, then, is a "pile of bricks"—meaningless, formless, chaotic.

But it is impossible for most of us to view it this way; we bring to bear on our perception of it the cargo—some public, some private—of knowledge, allusions, and images we carry around inside our heads. Adults are particularly laden with such cargo, the most basic being the concepts of time and space we use to structure reality. Lively is intrigued by the idea that the very young, as well as the primitive and the untutored, are not as fettered as adults by such mental cargo, and in virtually all her novels she does some speculating about the radically different way children look at the world. For example, Matthew's little daughter, Jane, we are told, lives in "the perpetual now of childhood, the interminable present from which, eventually, we escape and which we can never retrieve. . . . [Children] are in a state of original harmony with the physical world, knowing nothing and seeing everything. They roll with the planet, wake and sleep; their time is essential time, before it has become loaded with significance" (*CM,* 183). And the Victorian child Rose is twice removed from the cargo-laden adult outlook, first by virtue of being a child and second by virtue of being wholly without education. She is as close to perceiving reality raw as Lively can imagine: she is simply "a pair of eyes and ears, concentrated upon survival" (*CM,* 35); she does not know her own age, assumes she has always been here and always will be, and, lacking received knowledge, deduces from her own firsthand observations of daylight and night that the sun must move around in the sky.

At the other extreme, of course, are people like Matthew—and Lively herself—who carry in their heads an enormous amount of cultural and historical cargo. Matthew shares Lively's fascination with this whole topic and often wonders what it would be like to experience reality the way a child or a primitive person does. "Once," he muses wistfully, "people wandered through capacious and unstructured days, tipping only from morning to night, and season to season" (*CM,* 96). But Matthew, a protopyical modern man, is highly conscious of time, not only of the hours of the day but of the periods into which our culture has divided and segmented history. The narrator points out that people like Matthew see the city as "stratified. Decked out according to the times, furnished with costumed figures, with sedan chairs or hansom cabs. A chronology, a sequence," whereas objectively it is "without such constrictions. It streams away into the past; it is now, then, and tomorrow. It is as anarchic as the eye of a child." (*CM*, 76). Matthew frequently observes that for the educated eye the city is a coded narrative, a silent chronicle, a system of allusions.

The protagonist is thus fettered by the cognitive categories and received images of his culture, but at the same time he is aware of the arbitrary nature of these constructs. Like most of Lively's protagonists, Matthew has a number of experiences that expose to him this arbitrariness, moments in which he glimpses the anarchic, protean nature of reality and the fact that "time and space are illusory" (*CM*, 211). He is prone to those Livelyesque epiphanies we have witnessed in other novels, when chronological time suddenly seems suspended and one senses the simultaneity of all experience. "Everything is now," he thinks during one such experience, intuiting "that at some other point—at some unknown, unknowable then—he will have this time, this moment, in his head" (*CM*, 97). Even on an ordinary daily level Matthew sometimes experiences the elasticity of time and space. For example, driving through the city, he simultaneously registers the passing sights, attends to the radio news of other times and places, and weaves in and out of recent and more distant memories. He is thus "both here and now, there and then. He carries yesterday with him, but pushes forward into today, and tomorrow, skipping as he will from one to the other. He is in London, on a May morning of the late twentieth century, but is also in many other places, and at other times" (*CM*, 2).

Thus, although Matthew's perceptions of reality are by and large conditioned by his culture, he is capable of occasional anarchic moments. And paradoxically, although his historical consciousness is what causes him to segment reality into periods, it is also what enables him to perceive the simultaneity of all time, or the presence of the past. That is, whereas a primitive or a child would see just the aforementioned pile of bricks, Matthew, by an act of historical imagination, can perceive the resonances and associations of the pile. For example, driving through the old City of London, he glimpses "for a moment, in the mind's eye, a sequence of bodies toppling from buildings, squashed under brick and stone and timber—Roman slaves, squat medieval peasants, eighteenth-century labourers" (*CM*, 6).

What Lively is ultimately exploring in this novel is a variation of the old paradox about a tree crashing in the forest with no human being within earshot: the crash does occur, but in a sense it does not if no one is there to witness it. *City of the Mind* probes the same paradox about the reality of the past. On the one hand, the omniscient narrator presents historical episodes of which Matthew has no knowledge, thereby indicating that the past really happened; but on the other hand, Matthew continually presses the point that the past does not exist apart from human consciousness. "This city," he remarks to his colleague Tony Brace, "is entirely in the mind. It is a construct of the memory and the intellect. Without you and me it hasn't got a chance" (*CM,* 7). Lively does not resolve the paradox. This novel, then, presents her fullest exploration of the complex nature of reality, with its dual aspects of subjective and objective.

The "terrifying certainty of the stars"

City of the Mind begins and ends with mention of the stars, and the stars form a kind of symbolic backdrop to the novel, a reminder of the ephemerality and puniness of human existence in the face of the permanence and vastness of the universe. As Matthew himself puts it, "The world turns against the backdrop of this archaic reference system" (*CM,* 144). In Lively's other novels, characters only occasionally catch sight of this truth, usually during those moments of existential angst when they feel cut adrift from concrete, mundane reality; but in *City of the Mind* this perspective on humanity's insignificant place in the cosmic scheme dominates, in good part because of the abundant references to stars.

Matthew, more than usually prone to Livelyesque angst as a result of having been recently wrenched from the "safe warm capsule" (*CM,* 67) of marriage, is frequently awed by the mystery and massiveness of the universe, and it is usually thoughts or mention of the stars that trigger this reaction. In the very opening scene, for example, he is jolted by his daughter Jane's question, "Why are there stars?", to which "he has no answer" (*CM,* 1). Again, at a planetarium show, moved by the commentator's description of our galaxy as being merely one among millions of galaxies, all of them hurtling "for ever onward and outward into the darkness of the expanding universe," he wonders how, in light of this fact, human beings can carry on as though their lives were significant: this knowledge "should wonderfully concentrate the mind, and place one's own puny concerns within a proper context. Unfortunately, it does no such thing. Or, perhaps, fortunately" (*CM,* 84).

Contrary to what Matthew thinks, however, many people besides himself are subject to these same chilling insights into the flimsiness of quotidian reality as well as to the experience of feeling suddenly untethered from this reality. In ranging back and forth among the main narrative and the subnarratives, Lively highlights the commonality of these insights and experiences throughout the ages. For example, just after Matthew, walking through Covent Garden, notes that he feels existentially adrift now that he is no longer grounded by the familiar structure of marriage, the narrative cuts to little Rose, the nineteenth-century denizen of this same neighborhood, who has been catapulted into a similar state of disorientation, albeit by a different cause: "The child is ill. She is suspended in a timeless black sphere of pain, and fear, and solitude," "a blank and spinning existence that knows of nothing but its grief. . . . she is untethered, everywhere and nowhere, now and forever, a concentration of distress that is the world" (*CM*, 68).

Similarly, the episode in which Jane Halland accompanies her father on an outing to Greenwich is interspersed with frequent cuts to the subnarrative about Martin Frobisher, who embarked from this landmark on his voyage to the Arctic, and both Jane and Martin are shown to be experiencing the same insights into the elastic nature of time and space. Jane badgers her father with questions about why some days are long and others short and about where the hours go after we have used them, while Martin, having lost his bearings on uncharted seas, feels "adrift in a featureless sphere. There is up and there is down; there is north and south and east and west. But there is no here, and no there; they are untethered" (*CM*, 42–43).

The stars motif infiltrates and links together many such episodes, in which characters are suddenly existentially dislocated. For example, Matthew's thoughts about the "terrifying certainty of the stars" (*CM*, 45) and about their being "the one stability in lives of flux" (*CM*, 144) are echoes of Martin Frobisher's thoughts about the "blessed elusive certainties of sun, moon and stars" (*CM*, 122) in contrast to the uncertainty and fragility of the human lives aboard his ship. Similarly, World War II warden Jim Prothero, in the midst of battling the fire and destruction of the blitz, looks up at the "cold, perfect and inviolate" (*CM*, 117) stars and moon and is struck by their aloofness from the human turbulence raging below.

This frequent calling attention to the puniness and absurdity of human existence could easily result in a bleak novel, a Beckett-like portrayal of a human being as a paltry, ignoble thing. But on the contrary, *City of the Mind*, like Lively's other novels, offers an ultimately affirmative vision. Here as elsewhere, Lively suggests that despite the fact that hum. kind is a mere speck in a vast, indifferent universe, there is tran-

scendence and significance to be found in our experience. She demonstrates this primarily through Matthew, who, after falling in love, gradually regains the ability to experience those "silvered" (*CM,* 113), timeless
moments of happiness that stay lodged in the head and that seem to
weld one's spirit mystically to the physical spot in which they occurred,
moments that thus defy the ephemerality of human existence. The novel
concludes with a crescendo of such epiphanies and with Matthew's
apparent insight that these moments "of perfect grace" (*CM,* 219) are
almost mystically significant, serving as buoys in the chaotic, uncertain
sea of existence.

Therefore, in the very final scene, which like the opening scene presents a bedroom conversation between Matthew and Jane set against the
looming, symbolic backdrop of the starlit night sky, Matthew is able to
assert this vision and thereby ward off his daughter's terrified metaphysical anxieties. Having awakened in a panic, the child cries to her father,
"I didn't know where I was. . . . I was frightened. I thought I wasn't
anywhere" (*CM,* 219). She has articulated, of course, the existential disorientation Matthew himself—and numerous other characters in Lively's
fiction—is prone to. And yet he is able to reassure her of the concrete-
ness of her own existence. "Look," he says simply, pulling back the curtain for her to see the sky, "You're here, I'm here" (*CM,* 219–20). This
scene and this statement are emblematic of the paradox at the heart of
human experience and at the heart of this book: the spectacle of cosmic
vastness reminds us of the insignificance of our own existence; but at the
same time our daily experience—the experience of our fingertips, so to
speak—belies this fact. Furthermore, as Matthew and most of Lively's
other protagonists have discovered, the darkness and chaos of existence
can be redeemed by moments of epiphany and of human connection.

The Place of *City of the Mind* in Lively's Oeuvre

City of the Mind asserts more aggressively than any other Lively novel her
belief in the living presence of the past. Curiously, although the novel's
other main theme—the subjective nature of reality—is the one that the
title implies to be primary, what emerges most forcefully in the book is a
sense of the palimpsest quality of place, in this case, of the city of London.
Not since her children's novels has Lively so dramatically demonstrated
the way the lives of past inhabitants continue to reverberate in a place. In
most of her adult novels, she expresses this theme merely by pointing out
the physical and linguistic vestiges of the past—in the landscape, in archi-

tecture, in place names, and in dialect—but here, as in her juvenile fiction, she actually portrays the ghosts of past inhabitants and events as lurking invisibly in the midst of contemporary life.

This seemingly supernatural element, acceptable in children's fiction, may be regarded by some readers of *City of the Mind* as a flaw, inappropriate in an otherwise realistic piece of fiction. It is important to realize, however, that Lively's purpose is not to suggest that "ghosts," or mystical remnants of the past, actually exist, but rather to vivify her strong intuition that we are all shaped by our regional and cultural pasts. Whereas in her other adult novels she expresses this idea by having the narrator or a character observe the way the individual unwittingly betrays his or her heritage through speech and behavior, here she actually dramatizes the point. The phenomenon whereby the main narrative continually dissolves into a subnarrative, with the two being linked by an emotion or insight the protagonist and a character from the past experience in common, reveals the way the protagonist is unconsciously connected to a host of past existences.

Of all Lively's previous novels, the one that is thematically and technically closest to *City of the Mind* is *Moon Tiger.* That novel too demonstrates the weblike way the individual life is interwoven with other lives, past and present, and the way the past in a sense exists only in the mind of the individual contemplating it. Further, both novels employ expansive spatial and temporal scopes and innovative narrative techniques to explore these themes. Nevertheless, there are a couple of important ways that *City of the Mind* is more similar to its immediate predecessor, *Passing On,* than to *Moon Tiger* or any of the other works. In both her eighth and ninth novels Lively relies far less than previously on the kaleidoscopic method of narration and on the use of characters as mouthpieces for her ideas. Thus, although the same themes, with varying emphases, recur in all her novels, her technical handling of them is changing and developing, demonstrating that Penelope Lively continues to grow as an artist.

Conclusion

Penelope Lively is a consummate novelist. Her novels are artistically crafted and pared, and yet dense with ideas and rich in characterization. They satisfy at once the modern taste for spareness and Jamesian control of point of view and the old-fashioned taste for absorbing narrative and thematic "messages." Indeed, one of the most impressive qualities of Lively's fiction is the way it seamlessly blends a number of apparently divergent novelistic elements and strains: satire with authorial compassion for characters, realism with technical experimentation, comedy of manners with novel of ideas, and cozy, quaint settings with a radical questioning of reality.

She is also an unmistakably British writer. This is reflected not only in the idioms and expressions her characters use in abundance—the brisk "quite" and "sorry," the quaint "time out of mind" and "time was"—but in the way the author's sensibility seems to have been steeped in Britain's past. Her books are laced with allusions to and echoes of earlier writers and literary traditions—to Austen and the eighteenth-century concern with the relationship between nature and art; to Hardy and such Victorian concerns as fate and determinism; and to Woolf, Joyce, and Forster and the modernist interest in epiphanies and in narrative experimentation. Her novels are also resonant with echoes of Britain's historical past; they continually draw attention to the way earlier events and people are almost mystically embodied in the contemporary landscape. It is this awareness of the continuity between past and present that constitutes Lively's overriding thematic concern, different facets of which are expressed in different novels.

As preoccupied with the past as Lively is, though, she possesses a very modern sensibility and outlook. She has observed that a writer is inevitably permeated with the view of reality held by his or her own era and culture. She points out, "Even those novelists whose vision seems most detached from the realities of daily life are none the less bound up with it. We would not go to *The Waves* or *To the Lighthouse* for an evocative picture of early twentieth century English society, but equally no reader of any literary experience would suppose that they sprang from any other" ("Fiction and Reality," 3–4). The truth of this assertion is demonstrated by Lively's own fiction. Her agnosticism and its related existential anxiety; her belief that there is no objective reality, only versions of reality, and no objective self, only versions of self; her awareness of the tenuous nature of the constructs we use to give order and meaning to reality, particularly language and linear time—all of these are products of the contemporary philosophical outlook and all of these are embodied in Lively's fiction.

Examination of her work can thus yield rich rewards for students of the contemporary British novel. Her books suggest that, contrary to one widely held assumption, the postwar British novel has not retreated from the radical experiments with content and technique that characterized early twentieth-century modernism. Penelope Lively continues this experimentation. Beneath the quaintness and the polite Englishness of Lively's fiction lies a boldly contemporary vision of reality.

Notes and References

Chapter One

1. Penelope Lively, "Bones in the Sand," *Horn Book* 57 (1981): 648; hereafter cited in text as "Bones."

2. Penelope Lively, *Moon Tiger* (New York: Grove Press, 1987), 154; hereafter cited in text as *MT.*

3. Penelope Lively, *Treasures of Time* (Garden City, N.Y.: Doubleday, 1980), 35–36; hereafter cited in text as *TT.*

4. Penelope Lively, "Fiction and Reality: The Limitations of Experience," Walberberg Conference, organized by the British Council, Cologne, West Germany, January 1980, 6–7; hereafter cited in text as "Fiction and Reality."

5. Christina Hardyment, "Time out of Mind: Penelope Lively (née Low, St. Anne's 1951) Talks to Christina Hardyment," *Oxford Today* 2, no. 3 (1990): 31; hereafter cited in text.

6. Book Trust in conjunction with the British Council, eds., *Contemporary Writers: Penelope Lively* (London: Book House, 1988); hereafter cited in text as "Book Trust."

7. Neasa MacErlean, "The 'Nice' Penelope Lively," *Books and Bookmen,* November 1984, 28.

8. Helen Chia, "Lively as She Goes," *Straits Times* (Singapore), 4 June 1990, 2; hereafter cited in text.

9. In my June 1990 interview with her, Lively expressed her exasperation with critics who assume that if one is female and an author, then one must necessarily be writing about feminist or women's issues.

10. These books include the following: Randall Stevenson, *The British Novel since the Thirties: An Introduction* (Athens, Ga.: University of Georgia Press, 1986); Neil McEwan, *The Survival of the Novel: British Fiction in the Later Twentieth Century* (Totowa, N.J.: Barnes & Noble, 1981); and Malcolm Bradbury, *Possibilities: Essays on the State of the Novel* (London: Oxford University Press, 1973).

11. Penelope Lively, personal interview, 25 June 1990; hereafter cited in text as Interview.

12. Amanda Smith, "Penelope Lively," *Publishers Weekly,* 25 March 1988, 47; hereafter cited in text.

13. Penelope Lively, introduction, brochure accompanying traveling exhibition entitled *British Children's Literature 1900–1990,* sponsored by the British Council; hereafter cited in text as Exhibit Brochure.

14.   Penelope Lively, "Children and Memory," *Crosscurrents of Criticism: Horn Book Essays 1968–1977,* ed. Paul Heins (Boston: Horn Book, 1977), 228; hereafter cited in text as "Children."

15.   Keith Thomas, *Religion and the Decline of Magic: Studies in Popular Beliefs in Sixteenth- and Seventeenth-Century England* (London: Weidenfeld and Nicolson, 1971).

16.   Sheila A. Egoff, referring particularly to *Going Back,* labels Lively "the Proust of children's writers" (Sheila A. Egoff, *Thursday's Child: Trends and Patterns in Contemporary Children's Literature* [Chicago: American Library Association, 1981], 41; hereafter cited in text), and Eleanor Cameron compares *The House in Norham Gardens* with Woolf's *The Waves* (Eleanor Cameron, "The Eternal Moment," *Children's Literature Association Quarterly* 9 [1984–85]: 161).

17.   In arranging my discussion of Lively's stories, I have made the difficult decision to sacrifice depth for breadth, believing that most readers unfamiliar with her short fiction would prefer a survey approach rather than an intensive analysis of a select few pieces. Furthermore, because the stories are very varied in subject, tone, and narrative technique, I have for the sake of efficiency and organization divided them into categories. I hasten to point out, though, that nearly all the stories are more complex than my necessarily brief descriptions and my categorization method may imply. It is only the dominant feature of a story that has caused me to relegate it to a particular category; most of the stories contain additional features that overlap with other categories.

18.   Penelope Lively, "Corruption," *Corruption* (London: Heinemann, 1984), 17.

19.   Penelope Lively, "Pack of Cards," *Pack of Cards* (London: Heinemann, 1986), 297.

Chapter Two

1.   Penelope Lively, *The Road to Lichfield* (New York: Grove Weidenfeld, 1977), 35; hereafter cited in text as *RL.*

2.   Lively puts these words into David Fielding's mouth (*RL,* 28), but she has elsewhere made this point frequently, including in my interview with her, in Amanda Smith's interview with her (48), and in her article "Bones in the Sand," in which she states,

> You can know about the past but not sense the reality of the past; indeed, a great deal of present concern with the past obscures its immediacy. I think of television's treatment of the past as entertainment—in drama, in documentaries, too. Of the ways in which physical reconstruction of the past distorts it—the mannered look of historical sites, the textbook presentation of vanished landscapes. To be confronted with the authenticity of the past, to be jolted into understanding that the past is

true, people must see it in context: the Roman bricks of Cheapside laid bare by a German bomb, the shape of a human being etched into the desert sands. ("Bones," 642)

3.   Lively has stated, "We are all, collectively or individually, sustained by memory. In an individual, the disintegration of personality comes when memory goes: We are what we have been" ("Children," 229).

4.   She has discussed her interest in this theme in numerous interviews, talks, and articles, including my interview with her, Amanda Smith's interview with her (48), "Fiction and Reality" (21–22), and "The 'Nice' Penelope Lively" (28).

5.   Christopher Ricks, in a review of *The Road to Lichfield,* points out an additional pattern in the novel: the underlying literary allusion to Samuel Johnson, who grew up in Lichfield, and to his relationship with his father, whom he hardly knew (*Sunday Times,* 17 July 1977, 41).

6.   Penelope Lively, "The Writer as Reader," Cheltenham Literary Festival, Cheltenham, England, October 1988, 12; hereafter cited in text as "Writer as Reader." Lively explains how she had to do extensive research to acquire the archaeological knowledge needed to write *Treasures of Time.* Even so, she "trembled, when the book came out, lest [she] had committed howlers" and therefore "glowed with satisfaction" when she received the complimentary letter from Piggott ("Writer as Reader," 11–12).

7.   Susan Hill, "Steady Stuff," rev. of *Treasures of Time, Books and Bookmen,* September 1979, 23; hereafter cited in text.

8.   See Sir Thomas Browne, *Urne Buriall and The Garden of Cyrus,* ed. John Carter (Cambridge, England: Cambridge University Press, 1967), 7.

9.   In our interview, Lively spoke jeeringly of the way photographers from the magazine *Country Homes and Interiors* tried to make the interior of her farmhouse look more picturesque when they photographed it for a piece on Lively's life-style (Sylvia Howe, "At Home with Penelope Lively: Literary Tiger," *Country Homes and Interiors,* January 1989, 120–25). They rearranged furniture and added quaint touches to make the house accord with their readers' notion—rather than the reality—of an old-fashioned farmhouse.

10.   For example, Nellie says, "Nothing is as it seems" (*TT,* 149); Tom says, "Nothing is what it seems to be" (*TT,* 77); and Kate says, "Nothing is ever quite what it seems to be" (*TT,* 192).

Chapter Three

1.   Penelope Lively, *Judgment Day* (London: Heinemann, 1980), 3; hereafter cited in text as *JD.*

2.   Although most reviewers share my opinion that Sydney, Martin, and the other main characters are sensitive, complex creations, William Boyd argues that some of them are "drawn from stock. Mr. Porter behaves exactly as a crusty but kindly old codger should; the normally unforthcoming child responds to the affection and gestures of kindness, looks healthier, makes

friends with the Paling children and so on" ("The Skull beneath the Skin," rev. of *Judgment Day, Times Literary Supplement,* 21 November 1980, 1314; hereafter cited in text).

3.   Only one reviewer criticizes Lively for being too heavy-handed with this point, arguing that "fate's visitations [in *Judgment Day*] seem too crudely administered, a little too forensic" (Boyd, 1314).

4.   Marirose Arendale, rev. of *Judgment Day, Chattanooga Times,* 8 August 1981, B5.

Chapter Four

1.   For example, Brian Firth argues that an "inevitable limitation of the novel is the triviality of the central figures (whatever our own hypocrisies, we won't find them disturbingly revealed in this lot) and the forecastability of the narrative's development" and that "the situation is so thoroughly set up, and the central figures so transparent, that we can only wait for the inevitable moment when they are seen through" ("Chiaroscuro," rev. of *Next to Nature, Art, Tablet,* 1 May 1982, 430). Alan Brownjohn makes a similar criticism: "The targets are easy to set up, and Miss Lively hits them easily," and "*Next to Nature, Art* offers some shrewd comments on one interesting thread in the fabric of current English life; but the vehicle for them is this time rather crudely constructed, and they support a world-weary little message" ("The Heritage and the Hive," rev. of *Next to Nature, Art, Times Literary Supplement,* 23 April 1982, 455.

2.   Penelope Lively, *Next to Nature, Art* (London: Heinemann, 1982), 5; hereafter cited in text as *NNA.*

3.   Lively mentioned this in our interview as well as in her interview with Helen Chia (2). Also, in Lively's short story "A World of Her Own," the protagonist, who is the story's moral center, criticizes her artist sister for modeling herself after rude, irresponsible artists like Dylan Thomas and Augustine John rather than after unflamboyant artists like T. S. Eliot and Gustav Holst, who lived ordinary, responsible lives while still producing great art (Penelope Lively, "A World of Her Own," *Nothing Missing but the Samovar* [London: Heinemann, 1978]).

4.   In her unpublished lecture "Fiction and Religion," Lively holds forth at length about her view that fiction provides for the modern secular age the coherence, order, and enlightenment that religion has traditionally provided for those who believe in God (Penelope Lively, "Fiction and Religion," University Church, Oxford, 31 October 1990; University Church, Cambridge, 11 November 1990; hereafter cited in text as "Fiction and Religion").

Chapter Five

1.   Allan Massie, "The Mysteries of Life after Marriage," rev. of *Perfect Happiness, Scotsman,* 17 September 1983, 5.

2.   Penelope Lively, *Perfect Happiness* (Garden City, N.Y.: Doubleday, 1984), 112; hereafter cited in text as *PH*.

3.   Anthony Thwaite, "The Stuff of People's Lives," rev. of *Perfect Happiness, Observer,* 11 September 1983, 31.

4.   In "Fiction and Religion," for example, Lively states, "I call myself an agnostic, which implies inability to believe in a deity, rather than outright rejection of the very concept of a deity. I know that I can't believe in a god, and why I can't, but I accept that others can, respect their reasons for so doing without accepting them, and feel a curious combination of envy and wonder at the solaces available to them which are not available to me" (9). She made a similar comment to me in our interview, and then went on to say, "My husband, who is an agnostic, as I am, went not long ago to the funeral of a colleague, a professor of politics at the Catholic University of Dublin; he was a Catholic priest. He was one of a family of eight siblings, who all became priests and nuns. And Jack felt deeply envious of this absolute faith and belief he witnessed at the Catholic funeral Mass. I mean, I think we [agnostics] are right, we have the truth, but it would be easier to be [believers]."

5.   Lively herself finds such an anchor in art: in our interview she said that "one of the reasons novelists, some novelists, certainly agnostic novelists like myself, write is to attempt to find some kind of order where there appears to be none, to attribute some kind of meaning to a life which, in agnostic terms, apparently has no meaning."

6.   In our interview she talked about the strong, almost spiritual response she has to the physical world and about how frustrating she consequently finds its utter indifference. She also discusses this problem in "Fiction and Religion": "The difficulty, for me, lies with our relationship to [the physical world]—or rather, with our absence of relationship. The natural world is impervious; it neither knows nor cares. . . . are we to see it as a solace or a mockery? There is the world, looking as it does, functioning as it does, permanent and entirely unresponsive; here are we, sentient and caring, and entirely impermanent. What are we to feel about this?" (19).

7.   I am indebted to Professor Simon Gatrell of the University of Georgia English department for pointing out this connection.

Chapter Six

1.   Robert Taylor, "Crafting a Parallel Obsession," rev. of *According to Mark, Boston Globe,* 25 December 1985, 62.

2.   There are some striking similarities between this plot and that of A. S. Byatt's recent Booker Prize–winning novel, *Possession,* of which Lively has professed great admiration. Each of Byatt's two protagonists is, like Mark, a scholar researching the life of a deceased person of letters (a mid-Victorian poet and poetess, respectively). In similar fashion to Mark, these two scholars gradually move from a dry, academic interest in their work to an emotional identifi-

cation and obsession with their respective subjects as they are teased along by provocative gaps and silences in the biographical documents and ultimately uncover a secret love affair.

3. Penelope Lively, *According to Mark* (London: Heinemann, 1984), 110; hereafter cited in text as *AM*.

Chapter Seven

1. In our interview Lively provided some illuminating insights into her theory and taste concerning erotic scenes in fiction. She praised writers like Edith Wharton and Rosamond Lehman, who convey passion in concise, taut prose and elliptical, understated exchanges. In constructing her own love scenes, both in *Moon Tiger* and elsewhere, she has clearly been influenced by this approach.

2. Jean Ervin, "Did Penelope Lively Deserve the Booker Prize for 'Moon Tiger'?", rev. of *Moon Tiger, Star and Tribune* (Minneapolis), 27 March 1988, F10. This is one of the few negative reviews of the novel.

3. Lively mentioned in our interview that a number of male readers, including the novelist Julian Barnes, have even told her that they found themselves falling in love with Claudia while reading the book.

4. It is important to realize, however, that Claudia's and Lively's views of history are not synonymous. Lively's are somewhat more conventional. She explained in our interview that although she is interested in the subjective aspect of history—that is, in the nonchronological way we mentally experience it, with the wisdom of hindsight and with the cultural assumptions influencing our view—she would not go so far as Claudia in trying to incorporate this subjectivity into an actual history book. One of the reasons Claudia is so iconoclastic, Lively explained, is that in Claudia's day the academy's approach was very conservative: history was regarded as a series of political events that could be written about in an objective way, from the vantage point of the contemporary historian's superior understanding. This approach was current when Lively herself was at Oxford, and she found it inadequate. Since then, however, a more relativistic, history-of-ideas approach has taken over, in part as a result of the influential study discussed earlier, Keith Thomas's *Religion and the Decline of Magic*. But Claudia was writing history before these changes occurred and so felt a greater need to rebel than if, like Lively, she were writing today.

5. For a more detailed discussion of the feminist subtext of *Moon Tiger*, see Mary Hurley Moran, "Penelope Lively's *Moon Tiger*: A Feminist 'History of the World,'" *Frontiers: A Journal of Women Studies* 11, no. 2–3 (1990): 89–95.

6. Nancy Chodorow, "Family Structure and Feminine Personality," in *Woman, Culture and Society,* ed. Michelle Zimbalist Rosaldo and Louise Lamphere (Stanford: Stanford University Press, 1974), 59.

7. Roland Barthes, *The Pleasure of the Text,* trans. Richard Miller (New York: Hill and Wang, 1975), 47.

8.   Rachel Blau DuPlessis, *Writing beyond the Ending: Narrative Strategies of Twentieth-Century Women Writers* (Bloomington: Indiana University Press, 1985).

Chapter Eight

1.   Anita Brookner, "As Natural as Breathing or Going for a Walk," rev. of *Passing On, Spectator,* 8 April 1989, 33; hereafter cited in text.

2.   Victoria Glendinning, "Suitably Grave Matters," rev. of *Passing On, London Times,* 8 April 1989, 38–39.

3.   Sarah Gold, "Two Siblings Haunted by a Mother's Cruel Legacy," rev. of *Passing On, Newsday,* 30 January 1990, part 2, p. 6.

4.   Richard Bausch, "The Posthumous Power to Hurt," rev. of *Passing On, New York Times Book Review,* 11 February 1990, 12.

5.   Lively explained in our interview that although this statement of Woolf's provided the kernel idea for *Passing On,* she cannot pinpoint exactly where it appears in Woolf's oeuvre; she suspects she came across it in one of the diaries.

6.   Penelope Lively, *Passing On* (New York: Grove Weidenfeld, 1990), 20; hereafter cited in text as *PO.*

7.   Penelope Lively, *City of the Mind* (London: Andre Deutsch, 1991), 21; hereafter cited in text as *CM.*

8.   In our interview Lively expressed a similar skepticism concerning the Docklands enterprise.

9.   Virginia Woolf, *Mrs. Dalloway* (1925; reprint, New York: Harcourt, Brace and World, 1953), 9; hereafter cited in text.

10.   In her interview with Christina Hardyment, Lively explained, "I've just finished a novel [*City of the Mind*] . . . in which I've been trying to do precisely that—to make the point that the consciousness of the past exists only in the mind and the eyes of the beholder. It is a London book, about the past of a city: a literary expression of the sense in which the visual past of an object does not exist unless somebody looks at it with understanding. An eighteenth-century house, for example, has no meaning unless somebody is there to see it, to imagine it" (Hardyment, 31).

Selected Bibliography

PRIMARY WORKS

Novels

According to Mark. London: Heinemann, 1984; New York: Beaufort Books, 1985; Harmondsworth: Penguin, 1985; New York: Harper & Row, 1989.

City of the Mind. London: Andre Deutsch, 1991; New York: HarperCollins, 1991.

Judgment Day. London: Heinemann, 1980; Harmondsworth: Penguin, 1982; New York: Harper & Row, 1989.

Moon Tiger. London: Andre Deutsch, 1987; New York: Grove Press, 1988; Harmondsworth: Penguin, 1988; New York: Harper & Row, 1989.

Next to Nature, Art. London: Heinemann, 1982; Harmondsworth: Penguin, 1984.

Passing On. London: Andre Deutsch, 1989; New York: Grove Weidenfeld, 1989; Harmondsworth: Penguin, 1990; New York: Harper & Row, 1991.

Perfect Happiness. London: Heinemann, 1983; Garden City, N.Y.: Dial Press, 1984; Harmondsworth: Penguin, 1985.

The Road to Lichfield. London: Heinemann, 1977; New York: Grove Weidenfeld, 1991; Harmondsworth: Penguin, 1983; New York: HarperCollins, 1992.

Treasures of Time. London: Heinemann, 1979; Garden City, N.Y.: Doubleday, 1980; Harmondsworth: Penguin, 1986.

Short-story Collections

Corruption. London: Heinemann, 1984.

Nothing Missing but the Samovar. London: Heinemann, 1978.

Pack of Cards. London: Heinemann, 1986; New York: Grove Press, 1989; Harmondsworth: Penguin, 1987; New York: Harper & Row, 1990.

Children's Books

Astercote. London: Heinemann, 1970; New York: Dutton, 1971; Harmondsworth: Penguin/Puffin, 1987.

Boy without a Name. London: Heinemann, 1975; Berkeley, Ca.: Parnassus Press, 1975.

Debbie and the Little Devil. London: Heinemann, 1987.

Dragon Trouble. London: Heinemann, 1984.

The Driftway. London: Heinemann, 1972; New York: Dutton, 1973; Harmondsworth: Penguin, 1985.

Fanny and the Battle of Potter's Piece. London: Heinemann, 1980.

Fanny and the Monsters. London: Heineman, 1978.

Fanny and the Monsters (a collection of the three Fanny stories). London: Heinemann, 1983; Harmondsworth: Penguin/Puffin, 1982; London: Mammoth, 1991.

Fanny's Sister. London: Heinemann, 1976; New York: Dutton, 1979.

The Ghost of Thomas Kempe. London: Heinemann, 1973; New York: Dutton, 1973; Harmondsworth: Penguin/Puffin, 1984; New York: Berkley Books, 1986.

Going Back. London: Heinemann, 1975; New York: Dutton, 1975; Harmondsworth: Penguin/Puffin, 1986; Harmondsworth: Penguin (adult literature), 1991.

The House in Norham Gardens. London: Heinemann, 1974; New York: Dutton, 1974; Harmondsworth: Penguin/Puffin, 1986.

A House Inside Out. London: Andre Deutsch, 1987; New York: Dutton, 1987; Harmondsworth: Penguin/Puffin, 1989.

The Revenge of Samuel Stokes. London: Heinemann, 1981; New York: Dutton, 1981; Harmondsworth: Penguin/Puffin, 1983; London: Mammoth, 1991.

The Stained Glass Window. London: Abelard Schuman, 1976; London: Julia MacRae Books, 1990.

A Stitch in Time. London: Heinemann, 1976; New York: Dutton, 1976; Harmondsworth: Penguin/Puffin, 1986.

Uninvited Ghosts (a short-story collection). London: Heinemann, 1984; New York: Dutton, 1985; Harmondsworth: Penguin/Puffin, 1986; London: Mammoth, 1991.

The Voyage of QV66. London: Heinemann, 1978; New York: Dutton, 1979; London: Mammoth, 1990.

The Whispering Knights. London: Heinemann, 1971; New York: Dutton, 1976; Harmondsworth: Penguin/Puffin, 1987.

The Wild Hunt of Hagworthy. London: Heinemann, 1971; New York: Dutton, 1972 (as *The Wild Hunt of the Ghost Hounds*); Harmondsworth: Penguin/Puffin, 1984; New York: Ace Fantasy Books, 1986.

Nonfiction Book

The Presence of the Past: An Introduction to Landscape History. London: Collins, 1976.

Uncollected Nonfiction

"Bones in the Sand." *Horn Book* 57 (1981): 641–51.

"Children and Memory." *Horn Book* 49 (1973): 400–407. Rpt. in *Crosscurrents of Criticism: Horn Book Essays 1968–1977,* edited by Paul Heins. Boston: Horn Book, 1977. 226–33.

Foreword to *The Age of Innocence,* by Edith Wharton. London: Virago Press, Ltd., 1988.

Foreword to *A Father and His Fate,* by Ivy Compton-Burnett. Oxford: Oxford University Press, 1984.

Foreword to *Manservant and Maidservant,* by Ivy Compton-Burnett. Oxford: Oxford University Press, 1983.

Introduction to brochure accompanying British Council traveling exhibition, *British Children's Literature 1900–1990.* Sponsored by the British Council.

Unpublished Lectures

"Fiction and Reality: The Limitations of Experience." Walberberg Conference. Organized by the British Council. Cologne, West Germany, January 1980.

"Fiction and Religion." University Church, Oxford, 31 October 1990; University Church, Cambridge, 11 November 1990.

"The Writer as Reader." Cheltenham Literary Festival. Cheltenham, England, October 1988.

SECONDARY WORKS

Articles in Academic Journals

Batchelor, Judith L. "Not-Quite-Indexers in Fiction (and Non-fiction)." *Indexer* 14 (1985): 277–78. Discusses *According to Mark* in a survey of fictional and real-life characters with indexerly minds.

Cameron, Eleanor. "The Eternal Moment." *Children's Literature Association Quarterly* 9 (1984–85): 157–64. Discusses *The House in Norham Gardens* in a survey of children's time fantasy fiction; detects the influence of Virginia Woolf on Lively.

Chater, A. O. "Woodlice in the Cultural Consciousness of Modern Europe." *Isopoda* 2 (1988): 21–39. A hilarious article by an oniscologist (a biologist specializing in woodlice) who cites *Next to Nature, Art* and *A House Inside Out* in an analysis of how the treatment of woodlice in literature reflects a culture's attitude toward these creatures. Lively was tickled and delighted by this article, and subsequently included a reference to woodlice in *Passing On;* thus, an intertextual literary game of sorts concerning woodlice appears to be developing in Lively's fiction.

Halstead, Beverly. "A Novel." *Geologists' Association Circular* 886 (1991): 31. A brief discussion of Lively's interest in paleontology and dinosaurs, with particular reference to *City of the Mind.*

Langton, Jane. "Penelope Lively." *Dictionary of Literary Biography,* edited by Jay
    L. Halio. Vol. 14. Detroit: Gale Research Co., 1983. 107 vols. A dated
    but excellent survey discussion of Lively's novels, juvenile and adult,
    through 1982; also includes a biographical sketch.
LeMesurier, Nicholas. "A Lesson in History: The Presence of the Past in the
    Novels of Penelope Lively." *New Welsh Review* 2, no. 4 (1990): 36–38.
    Asserts that Lively's overriding theme is the living presence of the past in
    landscape and consciousness and demonstrates the various ways this
    theme is expressed in a number of her adult novels and children's novels.
Moran, Mary Hurley. "Penelope Lively's *Moon Tiger:* A Feminist 'History of
    the World.'" *Frontiers: A Journal of Women Studies* 11, no. 2–3 (1990):
    89–95. Argues that *Moon Tiger* can be read as a radically feminist novel
    that challenges and undermines established, patriarchal ways of repre-
    senting reality.
Rees, David. "The Narrative Art of Penelope Lively." *Horn Book* 51 (1975):
    17–25. Rpt. in *Crosscurrents of Criticism: Horn Book Essays 1968–1977,*
    edited by Paul Heins, 342–48. Boston: Horn Book, 1977. An earlier ver-
    sion of Rees's chapter in *The Marble in the Water* (see Rees below).
Smith, Louisa. "Layers of Language in Lively's *The Ghost of Thomas Kempe.*"
    Children's Literature Association Quarterly 10, no. 3 (1985): 114–16. Asserts
    that *The Ghost of Thomas Kempe* conveys to children a sense of the past not
    only through its presentation of time warps but also through its demon-
    stration of the way language changes over time.
Yvard, Pierre. "*Pack of Cards,* a Theme and a Technique." *Journal of the Short
    Story in English* 13 (1989): 103–11. A somewhat incoherent discussion
    (perhaps because of being translated from the French) of how Lively's
    body of short stories resembles a pack of cards, with each "card" portray-
    ing a different segment of English society.

Books Containing Discussions of Lively's Children's Fiction

Egoff, Sheila A. *Thursday's Child: Trends and Patterns in Contemporary Children's
    Literature.* Chicago: American Library Association, 1981. Scattered refer-
    ences to Lively's children's fiction, mainly noting their elements of
    fantasy.
———, G. T. Stubbs, and L. F. Ashley, eds. *Only Connect: Readings on Children's
    Literature.* 2d ed. Toronto: Oxford University Press, 1980. Scattered ref-
    erences to Lively's books in a thematically arranged analysis of modern
    children's fiction.
Landsberg, Michele. *The World of Children's Books: A Guide to Choosing the Best.*
    London: Simon & Schuster, 1988. An illuminating discussion of what's
    good and what's bad among contemporary and classic children's books,
    with high praise for Lively's work.

Rees, David. "Time Present and Time Past." *The Marble in the Water: Essays on Contemporary Writers of Fiction for Children and Young Adults.* Boston: Horn Book, 1980. Excellent survey of Lively's children's books, analyzing the way they express her interest in the continuity of the past; locates her fiction somewhere between history and fantasy.

Townsend, John Rowe. "Penelope Lively." *A Sounding of Storytellers: New and Revised Essays on Contemporary Writers for Children.* New York: J. B. Lippincott, 1979. Survey of Lively's children's books through *The Voyage of QV66,* followed by a statement by the author about her creative processes.

————. *Written for Children: An Outline of English-language Children's Literature.* 3d rev. ed. New York: J. B. Lippincott, 1987. Brief treatment of *The Ghost of Thomas Kempe, The House in Norham Gardens,* and *A Stitch in Time.*

Interviews, Biographical Articles, and Articles in Popular Magazines and Newspapers

Book Trust in conjunction with the British Council, eds. *Contemporary Writers: Penelope Lively.* London: Book House, 1988. A brochure containing a brief biographical sketch, an excellent overview of Lively's fiction by Anthony Thwaite, and a statement by Lively explaining her aims in writing fiction.

Chia, Helen. "Lively as She Goes." *Straits Times* (Singapore), 4 June 1990, 1–2. Excellent general discussion of Lively's life, personality, and fiction, written on the occasion of her June 1990 visit to Singapore as a guest writer at the Arts Festival.

Claffey, Charles E. "The Art of Lively." *Boston Globe,* 29 April 1988, 77. An account of an April 1988 interview in Boston in which Lively describes her childhood in Egypt and explains how she drew on this experience for *Moon Tiger.*

Connolly, Ray. "A Childhood: Penelope Lively." *Times* (London), 2 December 1989, 35. Fascinating, detailed description of Lively's childhood in Egypt.

Eastgate, Caron. "Books for Pleasure and Punishment." *Auckland Star* (New Zealand), 18 March 1987, B6. Brief discussion of Lively's life and fiction.

Hardyment, Christina. "Time out of Mind: Penelope Lively (née Low, St. Anne's 1951) Talks to Christina Hardyment." *Oxford Today* 2, no. 3 (1990): 30–31. Lively reminisces about her student days at Oxford and describes the genesis of her interest in history and memory.

Hart, Carolyn. "An English Gentlewoman at Home and Abroad." *Sunday Times* (London), 2 April 1989, G9. Discusses Lively's fiction, life, and attitudes, particularly her feelings about motherhood.

Howe, Sylvia. "At Home with Penelope Lively: Literary Tiger." *Country Homes and Interiors,* January 1989, 120–25. Life-style type of article with beautiful glossy photographs of the Livelys' farmhouse and gardens.

Levin, Angela. "At Home with Penelope Lively." *You,* 21 February 1988, 64–69. Another life-style piece with photographs.

"The 'Nice' Penelope Lively." *Books and Bookmen,* November 1984, 28. Describes Lively's interest in history, memory, and the relationship between biographer and subject, with particular reference to *According to Mark.*

Smith, Amanda. "Penelope Lively." *Publishers Weekly,* 25 March 1988, 47–48. An article based on Smith's interview with Lively, in which the author describes her childhood, her thematic concerns, and the way her husband and literary friends give her feedback on her work.

Index

The Author

Mary (Molly) Hurley Moran received her B.A. from Brown University and her M.A. and Ph.D. in English from the University of New Mexico. She has since taught at Clemson University in South Carolina and at the University of Georgia, where she is currently an assistant professor in the English component of the Developmental Studies Division.

Dr. Moran is the author of *Margaret Drabble: Existing within Structures* (1983); of articles on Drabble, Virginia Woolf, Oscar Wilde, Margaret Atwood, and Penelope Lively; and of articles and manuals concerned with composition and technical writing. Her research interests lie in the fields of modern British literature and composition studies. Her interest in Lively was spawned by a conference paper she wrote on *Moon Tiger,* which won the prize of best essay presented at the 1989 Carolinas Symposium on British Studies. A version of this essay was published in *Frontiers: A Journal of Women Studies.*